THE
Freezer
COOK
BOOK

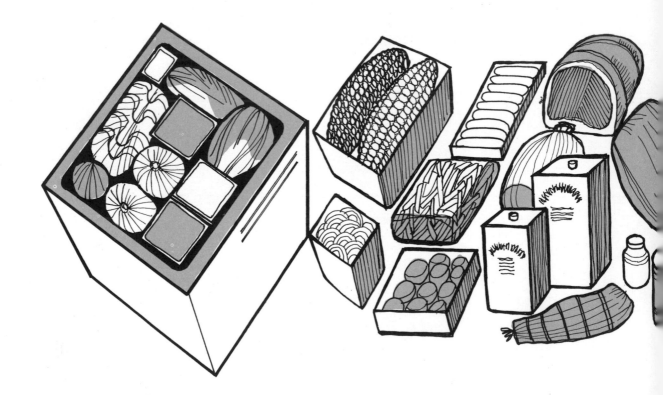

THE
Freezer
COOK
BOOK

by KATIE HASTROP

COLLINS GLASGOW and LONDON

Companion volume
MIXER COOKBOOK

ACKNOWLEDGEMENTS

I would like to express my sincere appreciation to all those people who have helped me through my years of enthusiasm for freezing.

To the Danish home economist who first attracted me to the benefits of the freezer some 12 or more years ago.

To the members of the Slape Home Freezer Club whose eager acceptance of my monthly newsletter gave the basis for this book.

To Stephanie Blasberg, Philips Electrical Ltd., and Betty Jakens, Kingsway Public Relations, for persuading me in the first place that I had something worth saying on the subject of Food Freezing, and subsequently giving constructive criticism on the manuscript.

To the home economists from the following organizations for their helpful comments and for permission to use the results of their latest research in this book:
Meat and Livestock Commission
Milk Marketing Board
Flour Advisory Board
White Fish Authority
National Dairy Council
Food Freezer Committee
Long Ashton Research Station
The many frozen food manufacturers.

To Pat Roberts for her tireless effort in deciphering and typing the manuscript and to Delia Clarke for checking of same.

Lastly to my husband for constant encouragement and support through the growing pains of authorship.

A list of Frozen Food Suppliers' names and addresses covering the whole country can be got from the Food Freezer Committee. 25 North Row, London, W1R 1DJ

Cover photograph by courtesy of Philips Electrical Ltd.

© Katie Hastrop 1972

ISBN 0 00 435520 2

First published 1972
Fourth impression 1976
Printed in Great Britain
Collins Glasgow and London

Contents

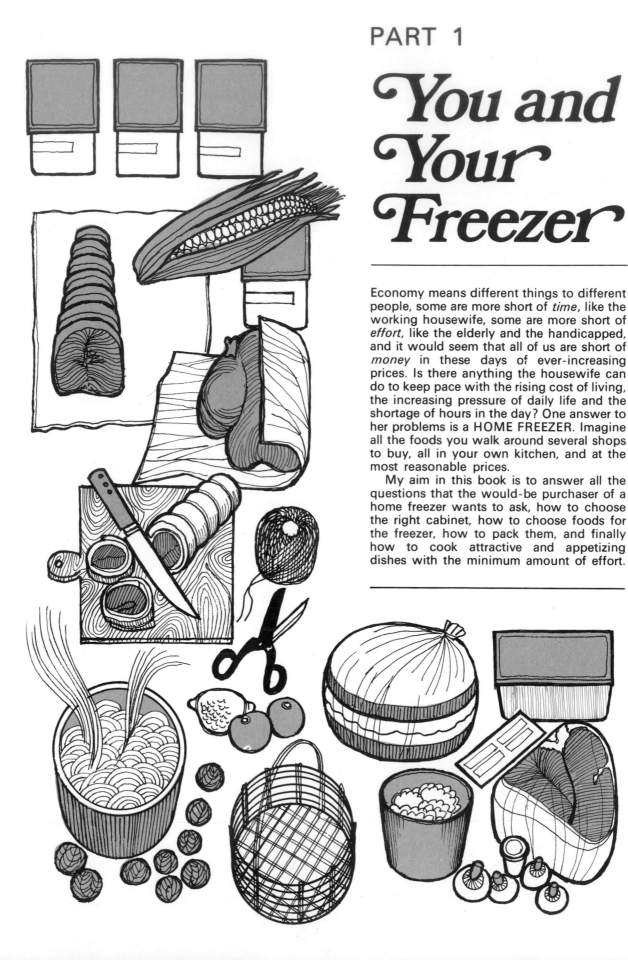

PART 1

You and Your Freezer

Economy means different things to different people, some are more short of *time*, like the working housewife, some are more short of *effort*, like the elderly and the handicapped, and it would seem that all of us are short of *money* in these days of ever-increasing prices. Is there anything the housewife can do to keep pace with the rising cost of living, the increasing pressure of daily life and the shortage of hours in the day? One answer to her problems is a HOME FREEZER. Imagine all the foods you walk around several shops to buy, all in your own kitchen, and at the most reasonable prices.

My aim in this book is to answer all the questions that the would-be purchaser of a home freezer wants to ask, how to choose the right cabinet, how to choose foods for the freezer, how to pack them, and finally how to cook attractive and appetizing dishes with the minimum amount of effort.

Who needs a Freezer?

EVERYONE needs a freezer. If you fit into any one of the following categories a home freezer should be high on your list of priorities; if you fit into more than one, you can't do without.

Productive gardens If you have a large productive garden giving you more fruit and vegetables than your family can cope with, the surplus can be packed in the freezer. But do *not* neglect the pleasure of eating the product fresh from the garden—so often new freezer owners are so keen to get their garden produce into the freezer, that they do not enjoy fruit and vegetables fresh.

Bulk food purchase I have devoted a special chapter to bulk-buying which I hope will help those who are buying in quantity for the first time. It is a great money saver. If you continue to buy the same commodities as before but in greater quantities, you can save 10—25% on retail prices. Lower prices for 'treats' like asparagus, steaks and prawns make it true to say that with a freezer 'it costs less to live better'.

People in a hurry A category in which many find themselves; no more fighting your way around crowded shops, no more battling to get the car into a convenient park. At last shopping becomes a leisurely pleasure.

Hostess with the mostest A lot of the pleasure of entertaining is lost to the housewife who finds herself tied to the kitchen. Complete menus for parties or weekend guests can be planned, prepared and stored in the freezer, so that she too can enjoy herself. Also the clever hostess can always produce a meal from the freezer when unexpected guests arrive.

A servant for mum Mum can cook when she feels like it, either a grand cook-in when she feels inspired, or just an extra portion or two during normal cooking. A mum with an army of hungry children during the holidays can prepare for the invasion and have time to share the children's pleasures. She can also leave food ready prepared for husband or children to simply cook through, so that she herself can have a day off.

Every day a holiday You can prepare picnic and sandwich meals for early start holidays, and a meal ready to pop into the oven on the return.

Out of season eating I really think we should enjoy foods in their season. But it is very nice to know that you can have green peas with your duck, crab with your salad, and blackberries with your pie at any time during the year.

The family of one For those living alone a home freezer eliminates the boredom of eating the same dish for three days running, yet makes it worth while making a stew or a curry, with two portions in the freezer for later in the month. For older people, a freezer could help with the cost of living on a fixed income, the problems of shopping in bad weather, and the lack of enthusiasm to ever be bothered to cook at all.

Rotten cooks Freezers are not only for good cooks: a whole host of gourmet dishes from Lobster Thermidor to Boeuf Strogonoff can be bought 'boil-in-bag' and are ready to serve in just 15 minutes!

The noble dieters It is easier to plan the dieter's food to fit in with the rest of the family menus when portions are set aside in the freezer. Those on special diets because of illness can also be more easily integrated into the family menus.

The real pay-off Last but not least, is the convenience of always having in the house the particular item of food you want, in perfect condition.

The How, What, Where & When

How big a freezer do you need? Always bigger than you think. A fair guide is 2—3 cu ft per person, but this depends on whether all meals are taken at home and whether a lot of entertaining is done. It is advisable to buy the largest you have room for and can afford, but if space really restricts you, you will just need to plan carefully.

Where can you keep the home freezer? Almost anywhere which is well ventilated and not damp. As you do not go to the freezer as often as the refrigerator it could be in a spare room, or garage. If you intend to freeze a lot of your own produce either from the garden or made dishes, it is easier if the freezer is in the kitchen. Do not put it next to the central heating boiler though, or it will have to work much harder to maintain its low temperature. If the freezer is to be in the garage make sure to buy one with a light inside the lid which comes on as you open it, or buy a miner's helmet with a lamp to find your way amongst the packages. It is also worth having a lock on your freezer since it is full of very desirable items.

What kind of freezer should you buy? The actual make will be for you to decide, but buy one from a recognized dealer with a reputation for good after sales service. There are two shapes of freezers on the market: the chest or dive-in type, and the upright. Food in an upright freezer is more accessible, so that you do not have to dive deep into a very cold chest, which is particularly significant if you are 5 ft 2 in or less! The upright freezer takes up less floor space, but you cannot pack quite so much per cubic foot as you can in a chest type of the same capacity. Sometimes the space between shelves of an upright freezer is not sufficient to take, for example, a large turkey, but unless you intend to have a lot of large awkward shaped packages in your freezer this is not usually too great a handicap.

In a chest freezer choose one with baskets, both suspended ones and ones on the base. Some freezers include several baskets, others you have to buy separately. If there are none available, use nylon string bags or coloured polythene bags to keep, for example, all the vegetables together.

Both upright and chest types are affected by Value Added Tax. Upright models are usually more expensive than the chest type of the same capacity.

Chest Type—more storage space per cubic foot, less loss of cold on opening, ability to take awkward shaped packages, possible work surface; cheaper to buy; cheaper to run.

Upright Type—packages more easily accessible, less floor space per cubic foot, work surface on smaller models.

Although it would seem that the advantages of a chest freezer outweigh those of the upright, the factors governing choice are often limited by unalterable conditions such as available space.

How much food will it hold? This depends very much on the size and shape of the packaging. Even sized boxes allow a great many more packages per cubic foot than awkward shaped joints for instance; however, for the same given space, the meat will weigh considerably more than, say, ten small boxes of black currants. It is some guide to say 20 lb per cubic foot, and after only a short time you will be able to judge just what you have room for. It is very important to underestimate the amount your freezer will hold when you place your first order for frozen food, just to be sure it will all go in!

How much will it cost to fill? It depends of course on whether you fill it with steaks and scampi, or fish fingers and beefburgers! It is worth remembering to have a little cash left over after purchase to buy food for your freezer.

Sometimes freezer suppliers help by giving a premium offer of £x pounds worth of frozen food of your choice. Do be careful not to get yourself tied to some scheme where your requirements are dictated by the supplier.

How much will it cost to run? This depends on where the freezer is situated, the temperature inside and outside the cabinet, and of course how many times it is opened. Upright freezers tend to cost a little more to run because the cold air drops out of the freezer as soon as the door is opened, whereas the cold air in the chest type has a job to actually come out of the top. I have not heard of anyone who has noticed any obvious increase in the electricity bill since owning a freezer.

Is there a difference between an ice cream cabinet and a home freezer? Yes, the ice cream cabinets, which are known as CON-SERVATORS, are designed to maintain a temperature of −18°C (0°F) which is perfectly adequate for storing already frozen foods, but not for freezing fresh foods.

The conservator is usually recognizable by its top opening flip-flop lid and is found in shops selling ice cream and commercially frozen foods. The thermostat is pre-set at the factory to maintain a temperature between −18°C and −20°C (0°F and −4°F) which only allows for pre-frozen foods to be stored. It is cheaper to purchase as its function is limited to storage only.

If relatively warm foods are placed in the conservator, the foods being stored at −18°C will be subject to a rise in temperature, thus in an effort to freeze the fresh foods entering the conservator the entire contents of the freezer are brought to a temperature above even storage temperature. It is not always easy to identify the conservator at first glance from small chest freezers with lift-off lids, and confirmation of the cabinet's capabilities should be requested from the manufacturer or retailer.

Can a freezer replace a refrigerator? No, their functions are quite different. The temperature inside a refrigerator is about −0°C (a temperature even above the freezing point of water) and the aim of the refrigerator is to keep perishable foods fresh for several days only.

Frozen food storage compartments in dual temperature refrigerators are often mistakenly called freezers. These refrigerators are cabinets with two doors giving access to two interior compartments. The lower one is a refrigerator with an adjustable thermostat allowing variable temperature control, the upper one is separately insulated and set at a low constant temperature (−18°C) and used like the conservator for the storage of already frozen food.

A* compartment maintains a temperature of approximately −6°C and will store frozen foods up to 1 week.

A** compartment maintains a temperature of approximately −12°C and will store frozen foods up to 1 month.

A*** compartment maintains a temperature of approximately −18°C and will store frozen foods up to 3 months.

A**** is freezer capable of freezing down fresh food.

If the compartment has no stars on at all, the temperature is above −6°C and is only suitable for ice-making.

How much fresh food can be frozen at one time? It is necessary to keep this within 10% of the total capacity of the freezer in any 24 hours. In a 4 cu ft freezer (allowing 20 lb per cubic foot), 8 lb of food may be frozen in 24 hours (10% of 4×20) and in a 12 cu ft freezer, 24 lb of food may be frozen in 24 hours (10% of 12×20).

If more than this amount is prepared for the freezer, which can quite easily happen if you purchase a whole lamb or half a pig or a large quantity of vegetables or fruit, then store that which is in excess of the 10% in the refrigerator overnight.

It is essential to cool food for freezing as quickly as possible before packing into the freezer. Make use of the refrigerator or cold running water to achieve this.

What preparation should be made for the freezer to receive the 10% load?
In many freezers a dial can be set to give lower temperatures, and in large cabinets there is often a fast (quick) freeze setting. This will give an internal temperature from −25°C to −30°C according to the maker's specification. When food is to be frozen the fast freeze switch should be depressed for several hours (24 hours if possible for maximum load) before use. The thermostat controlling the temperature inside the cabinet is then by-passed and the compressor works continually until the fast freeze switch is returned to its normal setting.

The fast freeze switch ensures that food already in the freezer attains such a low temperature that in the presence of the fresh food to be frozen it is not raised above −18°C. This lower temperature also speeds up the freezing process and the quicker the freezing the better the results.

The freezer may have a special quick freeze compartment which is either separately controlled or just an area sectioned off from the main body of the cabinet and consequently reaching the reduced temperature more quickly. The food to be frozen should be placed in this section if there is one, or against the walls and floor of the chest type, or directly on the evaporator coils which sometimes form the shelves of the upright models. After 24 hours the fast freeze switch should be returned to normal, and the food packed in the main body of the freezer, leaving the freeze-in section available for subsequent freezer loads.

Introducing single items
It is always desirable, but not necessary, to reduce the temperature before introducing single items like a loaf, or cake, or the odd half pint of sauce. However, these should be put near the floor or a wall of the freezer.

Why are particular temperatures chosen?
These are the temperatures judged to be the most efficiently economical for the purpose.
Home freezing temperatures of −25 °C to −30 °C are those which bring down the temperature of the food to be frozen, as quickly as possible. The quicker the lowering of temperature the smaller will be the ice particles formed in the food and the less damage to cell structure, and the better the results after thawing.
Storage temperature of −18 °C is considered to be the temperature at which food is given an adequate storage life. Lower temperature could be maintained at greater cost with longer freezer life, but the price paid for maintaining a lower temperature would be inversely proportional to the storage life.

What happens if there is a power cut?
If the freezer is full the contents will probably remain frozen for almost 36 hours, if only half full up to 24 hours, providing the freezer has **not** been opened allowing warm air inside. Resist the temptation to look and see if the food is all right.

A power failure will usually have been rectified during this time, but it is perhaps worth putting newspapers and blankets over the cabinet to insulate it if it is thought the failure may be lengthy. It is useful if a friend not suffering from the power failure has room in her freezer, or if you are on amicable terms with your butcher so that you can use his cold room. It is also possible to insure £50 contents for about £2 per year.

Much more likely than a serious power failure is the chance of switching off the power. Preferably do not have a switch plug, or, cover the plug with tape or a label DO NOT SWITCH OFF. Remember too that you no longer switch off the electricity at the mains when you go on holiday! You could have the freezer on a separate circuit.

If all the contents do begin to thaw you may refreeze again providing there is some evidence of ice crystals still present, or you may cook the uncooked items and then freeze, for in fact they are being frozen for the first time in their cooked state.

What is meant by 'never refreeze once thawed'?
The chances of any harmful effect to health in refreezing are very slight if normal kitchen hygiene rules are obeyed. It is bad practice (and bad household management) to be so badly organized that foods are being thawed and frozen many times and what will certainly be affected is the *quality* of the food, with a proportional deterioration on each occasion.

The O.K.'s
1. Raw foods from the freezer may be completely cooked and the resultant dish cooled, packed and frozen.
2. Those frozen foods which are removed from the freezer for thawing (especially if in the refrigerator) and are then not required may be put back in the freezer if some ice can be felt in the pack.
3. If a planned food preparation session can be organized with scrupulous kitchen hygiene the following are all right:

Cream may be thawed, still in the pack, in the refrigerator until defrosted enough to whip to piping thickness. Pipe selection of rosettes on to plastic tray, place open in the freezer to firm, then pack, seal and return.
Pastry may be thawed, still in the wrap, preferably in the refrigerator, until just thawed enough to roll out. Roll out and make pie crusts, tarts, pastry trimmings, *etc*, and refreeze quickly.
Cakes may be removed from the freezer, decorated whilst still frozen, and returned to the freezer.

The 'I wouldn'ts'
1. *Don't* take out cooked meats, particularly offal, thaw and return to the freezer, especially if no heat has been applied as with pâté, for instance.
2. *Don't* use frozen shellfish in a cold dish with no cooking, freeze and then return left-overs to the freezer, as with lobster mousse, for instance.

What is undesirable is to take food from the freezer, leave it hanging around in a warm atmosphere, allow it to come in contact with unclean surfaces, hands, equipment, *etc*, and then return it to the freezer only to freeze-in any contamination it may have collected during this time. It is the fluctuating temperatures that should be avoided; the middle temperatures, not hot enough to kill, not cold enough to inactivate, are the danger areas.

How often is it necessary to defrost?
Usually only once a year, when the contents are at their lowest. Just before the summer season's fruits and vegetables are ready to be harvested is often a convenient time.

If the freezer is used a great deal and is in a relatively warm place, frost may accumulate on the inside of the cabinet. It is as well to remove this as it appears, with a plastic spatula or scraper. If the frost is dealt with as it appears, a big defrosting operation may be avoided.

For complete defrosting, remove the contents; wrap the slow-thaw items in newspapers or a blanket, and put the quick-thaw dishes into the refrigerator which has been turned to its lowest setting.

Remove as much ice and frost as possible before it has a chance to thaw, using a scraper and a special dustpan and brush. Wash with lukewarm water. Dry with a clean cloth and set freezer to fast freeze to reduce temperature quickly before returning the food.

Do *not* try to accelerate the thawing by any mechanical means, and do *not* use a metal scraper which may puncture the walls of the cabinet.

Will anything and everything freeze? Yes, but whether the resultant foods are worth eating is for you to decide. It is always worth experimenting with small amounts, for several foods which earlier books said were not freezable are in fact quite successful, and some things are quite successful done commercially but are not so good home frozen.

Generally speaking, items with a high water content such as lettuce, cucumber and marrows are not good, but courgettes (baby marrows) in fact freeze very well. Melons bought commercially frozen are more successful than home frozen. Mayonnaise tends to separate, and hard-boiled eggs go leathery. And of course never occupy space with anything you don't particularly like.

Is it necessary to blanch vegetables? Yes, if you want to preserve the flavour, texture and colour over a long period.

Vegetables are blanched (scalded) to inactivate natural enzyme action by heat, so that they may be preserved for a year without the quality being affected. If blanching were not done the enzyme action would only be *inhibited* by the low temperature and not *inactivated* as it is by the high temperature of the blanching water.

It is worth experimenting by freezing some blanched and some unblanched vegetables, *e.g.* beans. Over a short period of a few weeks little difference may be detected, but over several months comparison is enough to convince.

Blanching timing (see page 22) is important, and should be strictly adhered to. If longer periods of time than those recommended are taken, then the vegetables will be virtually cooked, and if subsequently cooked for normal cooking time the product will suffer considerably, and yet it will be no fault of the freezer. All vegetables except corn-on-the-cob are best cooked from frozen, with as little water as possible.

When time is the important factor, as when the beans and peas are just right for the freezer the day before you go on holiday, then it is useful to be able to prepare them without blanching. They will not stick together when frozen, so quantities may be put into a large polythene bag (also saving time) when they resemble the commercially frozen free-flow packs. Remember to use these before the blanched ones, and they will probably be quite acceptable.

How long does food take to thaw? This depends on the texture and density of the item frozen. Meat, which is close textured, will take much longer to thaw than a sponge cake.

Pastry, most vegetables and fish are *best* cooked straight from the freezer. Joints, chops and steaks are able to be cooked from frozen, see page 18.

Thawing is best done slowly in a refrigerator, but will be quicker at room temperature, and in an emergency may be accelerated by placing the item, still wrapped or in its container, under the cold tap; not the *hot* tap, which would only succeed in part-cooking the outer surface.

How long will food keep? Chemical and physical changes continue to take place in food, but at a much reduced speed, whilst food is in the freezer. It is the effect of these changes that gives a freezer life of weeks, months or years, to different foods.

A guide to the keeping qualities of a wide selection of foods is shown. At the end of this stated time the food will still be perfectly edible. It will not become harmful to eat, but it will gradually lose flavour and texture.

Is there any loss in nutritive value in food that has been frozen? The freezing process affects food value very little, and freezing is by far the best method of preserving nutrients in food. Any loss occurs through the normal preparation of food and by the subsequent cooking.
Protein—little change in meat, fish, *etc*, whether it is frozen cooked or uncooked.
Fats—go rancid at temperature above $0°F$ ($-18°C$) and if stored for long periods. Vitamin A is destroyed if fat goes rancid.
Carbohydrates—nutritive value stays the same.
Minerals—are sometimes lost in thawing when discarded in the drip. One should aim at reducing the drip by quick freezing or by using the drip in the cooking process.
Vitamins—any loss of vitamins is due to preparation or cooking and not to low temperature storage. In efficiently prepared food for the freezer, as in commercial freezing where all necessary conditions can be met, there may be a greater retention of vitamins than in freshly prepared foods. Vitamin C (ascorbic acid) retention is often taken as the criterion of value of frozen food. The freezing process does *not* affect this vitamin, which is, in fact, added to some fruit to prevent discolouration (see page 27).

10

Packaging for the Freezer

Why do we need to pack? Careful packaging is essential, firstly, to preserve maximum flavour and maintain a good textured product without discolouration; secondly, to prevent flavours and odours being transferred; thirdly, it is necessary to give care to the packaging of decorated or soft foods so that the shape is not damaged during storage in the freezer. Special care must be taken with irregular shaped packs, *e.g.* poultry and joints of meat. It may be necessary to protect with additional over-wrap any protruding bone or sharp surface that may puncture or damage another package in the freezer.

Packaging *must* prevent dehydration in the freezer. It is sometimes difficult to appreciate that drying-up can take place even at sub-zero temperatures. When this happens to food in the freezer it is known as Freezer Burn, and can be recognized by a discoloured dried-up looking surface which in bad cases can almost be powdery when rubbed. It is obvious that a drying out of juices in fruit, vegetables, meat, poultry, *etc*, is going to have an adverse effect on the taste of the product when cooked. It is worth saying here that freezer burn does not represent health hazard to the consumer, only that the taste will be inferior. Sometimes frozen chickens with an exceptionally dried up skin are sold very cheaply because of freezer burn, but providing they are casseroled or curried in a well flavoured sauce they are worth buying if they are particularly cheap.

How do we achieve good packaging? All wraps and containers must be moisture and vapour proof, and as much air as possible must be excluded from the package. As liquids expand on freezing (water expands about 10%) about 1 inch headspace should be left or the container will burst in the freezer. For this reason milk cannot be frozen in the bottle. All wraps and containers must be sealed well. Good packaging gives extra space in the freezer and makes identification of products easier. The packaging material itself must be free from taste or smell and, of course, be non-toxic; it must also be non-fragile at low temperatures, and not become brittle or crack. It must not stick to either the body of the freezer or other packages.

So what can we use?

Polythene: both bags and sheet polythene are probably the most used and useful material for freezer packaging. The thicker the polythene the better, but if too thick it is difficult to handle and bulky to use, so look for the recommended gauge of 120–150 on the packets. It is worth having a supply of polythene bags of all sizes, including gusseted ones for the packaging of large and awkward objects. The very thin clinging polythene is good as an underwrap but the packet should be further protected for low temperature storage. Polythene bags are useful for most foods,

but not so easy for use with liquids. Use them as liners for good straight sided containers, removing them from the container when frozen. In this way a relatively small selection of plastic boxes, *etc*, may be used for shaping, and discarded after use.

Experimental work is being undertaken at the moment with a special polythene bag, in which vegetables and cooked dishes may be packed and frozen in the bag, and reheated, like their commercial equivalents straight from frozen, in a pan of boiling water.

Plastic: all sizes and shapes of both rigid and flexible containers with tight-fitting lids are useful. Remember that square-shaped are easier to stack and take up less space in the freezer. Tests show that twice as much (by weight) can be packed in the freezer when straight-sided containers are used instead of the round tub types.

Aluminium foil: ordinary household foil is not thick enough to withstand low temperature storage, so double thickness should be used. A heavy-duty foil is now on the market which is 40% thicker, and may be used singly. Foil is particularly good for moulding around awkward shaped packages. As aluminium is a good conductor of heat the package will freeze more quickly, making it a very satisfactory freezer material. However, it can be attacked by acids in the food which make small holes in the foil during storage, therefore foods with high acid content, or dishes containing vinegar or lemon juice should not be packed in foil. As foil punctures fairly easily it is as well to overwrap with polythene.

Shaped foil dishes: there is a magnificent selection of foil containers (some with fitted lids) on the market suitable for almost every occasion. The great advantage of these is that they may be placed in the oven straight from the freezer and are therefore ideal for pies, tarts, cooked dishes, *etc*; again avoid use with acid content foods.

Using these containers, complete dishes may be prepared for the freezer, thawed, reheated and served in the same container. Foil moulds with snap-on lids are also available in ring, bell and heart shapes, which allows moulded dishes to be stored in the freezer without the problems of un-moulding and then packing for the freezer with possible damage to the shape.

Aluminium foil may be used to line a favourite casserole or pie dish, thus shaping your own container. The wrapping can then be peeled away from the still-frozen food which may be reheated and served in a dish that you know it will fit.

Foil bags, rather like the old-fashioned blue sugar bags, are also available. They are easy to fill and keep a good shape for packing.

Waxed cartons: these are quite suitable for the freezer. Although they are re-usable they stain badly, making it really necessary to line them with polythene, in which case you might just as well use a throw-away packet like a sugar or cereal box. Again the straight-sided ones are better for storage when not in use. Unless they have a snap-on or screw lid these cartons need sealing with freezer tape.

Freezer paper: this may have a waxed or plastic film coating and can be used to parcel products for the freezer and it is particularly useful for separating several items in one package, *e.g.* a small piece between each chop in a large parcel of chops makes it much easier to remove one or two as desired.

No-cost packaging for the freezer: this is, of course, not strictly accurate, as the commercial products in containers suitable for re-use in the freezer, are probably a little more expensive because of the packaging, but it seems economical!

Cottage cheese, yogurt and margarine cartons may be used. If these containers do not have a re-usable lid they can be covered with foil. Among the most useful containers for the freezer are the individual jam pots many hotels and restaurants use. These are particularly handy for small portions of apple sauce or chopped herbs. A well washed washing-up liquid container proves useful for storage of home-made biscuits if you adapt the top with freezer tape to form a hinge.

Glass: not really a very good product for the freezer as most glass tends to shatter at low temperatures. One can experiment by placing a glass jar filled with water (leaving 1 inch headspace) in a polythene bag. If the glass does shatter at least all the fragments will be contained within the polythene bag and only water will be lost and not expensive sauce! It is particularly important to leave the headspace, for whereas the snap-on lid of a plastic container will just pop off if the liquid expands, in a screw-top glass jar this cannot happen and therefore the sides of the glass must go. Do not use narrow necked jars (like sauce bottles) for they are more likely to crack because of the restricted space. It is as well to thaw slowly items stored in glass containers in the refrigerator as quick changes in temperature make cracking more probable.

For short-term storage, glass serving dishes may be placed in the freezer. Thick glass is safer than thin, and the ovenproof type is usually all right if the return to room temperature is slow. The disadvantage of storing liquids in glass containers is that complete thawing is necessary and cannot be accelerated by immersing in water or by easing out as can be done with the flexible plastic containers.

Cardboard: both boxes and cut-out circles of cardboard are useful for protecting easily damaged food in the freezer. Items like sponge cakes and pastry flan cases can have their sides broken or squashed by pressure from other packages if not protected. Either place cake, *etc*, on a cardboard circle which is slightly larger than cake, then wrap in foil or polythene, or wrap first and place in box for storage in the freezer.

Overwraps: Nylon stockings, newspapers, mutton cloth, are all suitable when additional wrapping is required.

Not suitable for freezer packaging:
(a) Greaseproof paper which is not moisture-proof and allows considerable dehydration even over short periods.

(b) Unwaxed cardboard without additional lining or overwrap.
(c) Expanded polystyrene which acts as an insulator and therefore slows up freezing process.
(d) Tin cans which psychologically are associated with ordinary shelf life and may be accidentally removed from freezer storage.

Important criteria for freezing packaging
(a) That it should be reasonably priced and so not add too great a cost to the product being frozen thus making the procedure uneconomical.
(b) That consideration be made for the storage of packaging when not in use; it is ill conceived to lose valuable space in the kitchen for the storage of empty containers, yet you do not want it in an inaccessible place (*e.g.* shelf in garage) as if you are using the freezer to its maximum potential, you will have frequent need of containers.

Removing the air: Whilst it is extremely important to endeavour to remove as much air as possible from the package before freezing, the withdrawing of air by sucking through a straw is not recommended. It is quite possible that more harmful substances will enter the package should you accidentally blow and not suck. It is also possible, when sealing a number of bags, that the end of the straw or glass tube which has been in the mouth would get reversed and go into the bag— both possibilities being far worse for the food than the small amount of air that has not been excluded!

It is possible to exclude more air if packaging is done in water, but this is only practical with items like meat or poultry. Place the joint of chicken in the polythene bag, immerse the bag in bowl of water, smoothing the polythene over the surface of the contents (not allowing any water to enter bag), remove and seal, and wipe surface dry.

Sealing
(a) Freezer tape which is specially treated to be adhesive at low temperature is necessary; ordinary Sellotape is not suitable. This tape may be transparent or opaque, and different colours, and it is sometimes possible to write on the opaque type, so eliminating the need for additional labelling.
(b) Builders' masking tape is also suitable for use in the freezer.
(c) Twist seals, paper or cellophane covered wire are easier for sealing polythene bags than the longer and thicker plastic covered wire. Ensure that sharp edges are turned over to prevent perforation of adjacent packages.
(d) Rubber bands tend to perish over long term storage.

Heat sealing: polythene may be sealed by using the edge of an electric iron set at its lowest setting, protecting the polythene by two sheets of tissue paper. The same result can be achieved by using curling tongs and if a great deal of freezer packaging is done this way it may be worth investing in an electric sealer specially made for the purpose.

Labelling: this is extremely important in the freezer as several products lose their visual identity when frozen and mistakes like tomato sauce instead of raspberry purée can have disastrous consequences!

As much information as possible should be written on the label including contents, number of portions, date frozen, and if possible best method of thawing or cooking. For example:

```
Date
2 portions Minced Beef with Gravy
Re-heat
From frozen—25–30 minutes
    Gas No. 8 or 450°F (232°C)
If thawed—15–20 minutes in pan
```

For vegetables or fruit an indication of the variety, and whether blanched or unblanched, in sugar or syrup, *etc*, will all prove useful information.

Stick-on labels which remain adhesive at low temperatures are suitable for flat surfaces, tie-on labels are best for polythene bags. The lids of some of the foil containers have a white card surface suitable for writing direct on the package, and it is worth buying extra lids if any containers are to be re-used. The information may be written on ordinary note paper, then covered completely with transparent freezer tape as it is applied to the container.

Marking: ink or ball point disappears after storage at low temperatures, therefore felt-tipped pens, wax crayons or chinagraph pencils should be used.

Record book: one should attempt to keep a record book of items both in and out of the freezer in order to use items in correct rotation and to assess the quantities used and required. I think it is fair to say that those with well organized refrigerators and storecupboards will soon evolve a system of freezer use and identification, whilst those whose cupboards and drawers are in a permanent state of turmoil will find it difficult to be different in using a freezer.

No system is dogmatically right and the one which works for you is the best to follow whatever books or well-meaning friends try to tell you!

Bulk-buying

New freezer owners are often somewhat overwhelmed at the thought of filling the freezer with what might amount to 200–300 lb of food. How do you start to think *big* in terms of shopping for your freezer? How can you know how many peas, ice creams or fish fingers your family is going to consume? You should not rush to fill the freezer, but stop, consider and shop around.

GENERAL POINTS

Perhaps most important, the food you buy is not a bargain unless you need it. So often people buy items just because they are cheap. Be selective on the basis of previous experience of family likes and dislikes. At the same time there will be the opportunity to buy some foods that you may never have tasted before, so buy *one packet* or *one bag*, and taste before buying in quantity.

If possible buy what are known as free-flow or shatter packs of fruit, vegetables and items like prawns. This will enable small quantities to be removed from the pack as required before returning the bag quickly to the freezer. Where possible, buy individual portions as you may find it difficult to remove say, a herring, from a 3 lb block. Some items are only available in block form and a freezer knife will prove useful in cutting off required amounts.

When a box of say two dozen chicken portions or steak or chops is purchased, remove a few, re-wrap and store in freezer baskets for easy access, leaving the remainder stored in the base of the freezer until required.

If when you usually eat fish you fry it in egg and breadcrumbs, then buy the product ready crumbed. When the occasional recipe requires the fish uncrumbed wash off the coating. If you more often serve fish in a sauce buy the uncoated fish and have breadcrumbs in the freezer ready for use.

If the manufacturer has put instructions for thawing or cooking on the pack, it is as well to follow his advice: it represents a lot of test work done in the home economist's kitchen especially for your benefit!

What is bulk-buying? It is the economics of getting items at a reduced rate because you have bought in quantity, usually accepting that you will do without some of the refinements of retail shopping, like individual service, personal delivery, credit account, *etc*.

Where can you buy bulk? Almost anywhere. There are very few places that won't be prepared to come to an arrangement with you if you are prepared to buy in quantity.

The market stall This mostly applies to fruit and vegetables, and the rule of only buying really fresh produce still applies, but sometimes if bad weather has kept customers away or a delivery arrives too late in the day, the stall holder will be pleased to give you a reduction even if his profit margin suffers.

The market gardener Do not always expect to save money here but usually the produce grown by the small market gardener is of good quality and so worth buying to freeze if you are unable to grow your own. Sometimes a market gardener will grow certain vegetables especially for you if he knows he has a guaranteed customer.

The farmer Fruit, vegetables, meat and poultry may often be bought direct from the farm.

Although here the product may be of good quality, it may also prove expensive if one takes into consideration all the preparation for home freezing that is necessary.

Questions one must evaluate in relation to the price asked are: are the fruit and vegetables young/fresh enough for freezing, have you to pick your own (see page 21), will the meat be hung for the recommended time, if not where could you hang it, will the joints be cut, will the poultry be drawn and trussed?

The butcher Both the butcher you know, and the one you don't, may be sources of meat for your freezer.

It is important to know a little of the meat trade's economic planning before negotiating the purchase of bulk supplies of meat. The butcher buys meat at xp per pound for the whole animal, which means he pays exactly the same for the bone, fat and gristle as he does for both the best and the cheaper cuts of meat.

Your own butcher may order an extra carcass from his wholesaler for you, and if you are to home-butcher it yourself he may not charge you much in excess of the price at which he was able to buy. It is *you* then, who is paying for all the above throw away products at the same price as the actual edible meat, and it is estimated that this can be anything from 10–20% depending on the animal. For really rewarding meat to come from the freezer it is important that you learn something of butchering (see pages 16–17).

Perhaps more usual with family butchers is for the freezer owner to purchase either the whole animal (or half or quarter of the animal) cut by the butcher to her special requirements, or for the housewife to buy meat packs of cuts of beef, lamb or pork considered by the butcher to represent a good selection of the product for all types of cooking.

In either of these cases the butcher has spent his time and skill preparing the meat and must of course add the cost of this to the price of the meat. It is usually expressed within the price per pound paid for the meat. Even allowing for this charge and the waste from bones, gristle, *etc*, the price per pound is usually well under the price of the retail equivalent. One must accept that included in the meat packs are some of those cuts which are always cheaper, *e.g.* stewing beef, breast of lamb, belly of pork, *etc*. These are all delicious if cooked properly, so you must look for recipes using the cheaper cuts and not be too critical of their inclusion in the pack.

The variation in retail price of the differing cuts of meat is determined by both supply and demand. The butcher must cost his meat so that he will not be left with excess of any particular cuts. It is obvious that with only 2 lb of fillet in up to 300 lb of beef, it has to be expensive to reduce the number of customers fighting for it; similarly there are only two or three leg chops from each leg of lamb. This means that you will find the normally expensive cuts of meat are to be bought cheapest in the poorer parts of the city, where the demand for them is lower, conversely the so-called cheaper cuts are probably at their cheapest in the best areas of the city where demand for them is less.

The Supermarket Almost every week in the large supermarkets there are the loss leaders. These are the items that are low in price and their value for money is well publicized over the store's windows in order to attract you into the store.

With a freezer at home the housewife may take advantage each week of differing loss leaders. These are often most worthwhile in the meat section. Shoulders of lamb at dramatically reduced prices is a familiar sign, as are similar posters telling of bargain offers in poultry. These will, of course, usually be already frozen and all they will require of the freezer owner is her speedy return home so that the time between leaving the refrigerated cabinet of the supermarket and entering the freezer is as short as possible.

Other Retail Food Shops If you have become accustomed to buying in any of the above situations, you will soon pluck up courage to ask for a reduction for quantity buying; it may not always work but worth trying all the same.

Cash-and-Carry Depots These have been available to the bona-fide caterer for some years, but with the growth of the home freezer market some are now allowing all to enter. For those who are not able to be at home for a delivery of frozen food the cash-and-carry is very useful, but it is important that one doesn't delay getting the food home and into the freezer. It is also useful to have either an insulated box in the car or at least lots of newspaper to help keep the food as cold as possible. Insulated boxes made of expanded polystyrene can be purchased, or may be home-made by lining a cardboard box with polystyrene off-cuts.

These establishments are organized to work with minimum staff so do not buy too many heavy items unless you are able to carry them.

For the purchase of frozen food it is best to go to a cash-and-carry specializing in the sale of food for the freezer. Check also the loading line on display freezers, ensuring that all frozen food is packed below this line.

In the general purpose cash-and-carry one can often take advantage of extra large catering cans of fruit which may be opened and repacked in containers suitable for the freezer, thus representing both a considerable saving in money and the convenience of small quantities in the freezer.

Other products that may be repacked for the freezer in this way are soups and fruit juices, but I would rather not freeze any canned cooked meat or fish.

The frozen food distributor For the purchase of commercially frozen food for your freezer, the specialist is always the best source.

Firstly, choose a supplier who already has a well established trade with the caterers in his area, for this ensures that his turnover of food is rapid, and eliminates the question that is often asked when calculating the freezer storage time 'How long has it been stored at the depot?'

Secondly, choose a supplier who delivers in a refrigerated van. You may be last on his delivery list, but your food should be in just the same condition as if you were first.

Thirdly, choose a supplier who really knows

about frozen food and home freezing, so that you can buy with confidence, and discuss with him any problems that may arise. Do not get involved with any sales schemes that tie either you or your money to one supplier. You must be able to purchase how and where you like, and it is the responsible supplier who will always prove the most satisfactory in the end.

When the supplier offers a free delivery service get into the habit of ordering say a £5·00 order once a month rather than a £25·00 order once a quarter. In this way the stock in your freezer gets turned over more quickly and a better rotation of the contents is ensured. With organized monthly deliveries you can check the contents of your freezer more often.

Having established the day of delivery from the supplier, organize the space in your freezer to receive its new load. And most important, do not be out. The van driver is on a carefully timed and costed delivery round, and a return visit means more time and more petrol, and it could well be a major factor in deciding prices when the distributor reviews his costs.

If something is wrong with the food ordered or the quality of the products is not up to standard, register your complaint straight away.

The following information tells you something of the commercially frozen products available. It will be seen that amongst them are some foods that it is not possible to home freeze satisfactorily, but with the special resources available to the frozen food industry these difficulties have been overcome. New products appear every month.

Fruit: Raspberries, strawberries, bilberries, blackberries, black currants and red currants, are available in free-flow packs of either 1 lb, 2 lb or 5 lb which means that small amounts may be removed from the bag and the pack returned to the freezer. Apples, fruit salad and melon balls are usually sold in 2 lb bags and packed in syrup. Apricots, peaches and pineapple slices are usually in 1 lb packs.

Excellent home freezer purchases are concentrated orange and grapefruit juices which have the real taste and food value of fresh oranges and grapefruit, and find many uses in cooking.

Vegetables: Like fruit, many of the vegetables are in free-flow packs making it easy to remove a small amount and return the pack.

The exceptions to the free-flow packs are asparagus and broccoli which are packed in 2 lb boxes. The asparagus spears can often be separated by gently easing with a knife.

Mixed vegetables containing sliced beans, carrots, sweet corn, peas and broad beans are a colourful addition to a meal. Mushrooms, although best home frozen in butter, are successfully commercially frozen without butter and available in 2 lb free-flow packs. Corn-on-the-cob is always individually frozen (and should be thawed before cooking) and two cobs are usually sold together in a pack.

Available at the moment only in retail packs are delicious tiny onions in white sauce, ratatouille (a mixture of unusual vegetables), but it is possible to buy 2 lb free-flow packs of diced green and red peppers.

Peas and Brussels sprouts are available in three grades, usually small, standard and medium.

Dairy Produce
Cream is the most popular dairy product for home freezer owners, as the price is considerably less than if purchased retail, and the convenience of always having it available is an added pleasure.

For adding to soups, sauces or whipped for mousses, soufflés, *etc*, the small 4 oz jars of dairy cream are excellent. They need to be completely thawed (about 2 hours at room temperature) so that they may be poured from the jar with ease.

For whipping or piping consistency for decorative work, the dairy cream sold in polythene sachets of 10 oz and 1 pint is the best. Although this is the same cream that is in the small jars, it can be whipped much thicker. When only 1 pint sachets are available a portion may be sawn off with the freezer knife and the remainder returned to the freezer.
Jersey cream is usually sold in ½ or 1 pint waxed cartons.
Clotted cream is sold in 4 oz jars.
Ice Cream of various flavours is available in normal retail packs, or the more popular ½ and 1 gallon packs. Commercial ice cream should have a storage life of up to 3 months.
Mousse: Strawberry, raspberry, chocolate and lemon are available in individual portions.
Yogurt: Most of the popular fruit yogurts are now available frozen.
Dairy cream products: These include the delicious dairy cream sandwich cakes which are useful to have in the freezer as they thaw quickly. They also provide the basis of many imaginative desserts (see pages 72 and 82). Chocolate eclairs filled with fresh cream are also a favourite; they come individually wrapped in boxes of thirty-six. Sponge and ice cream rolls provide a basis for exciting desserts (see page 77). Both individual and larger sized trifles can be bought ready made and decorated.

Meat, Poultry and Meat Products: Meat is purchased either as selected cuts to form packs or in catering boxes of portion controlled lamb chops, pork chops, steaks, *etc*.

Important Note If a meat pack is to be purchased from a supplier, ascertain that this will be delivered to you already frozen, for it will always represent a fair weight and your freezer may not be capable of freezing anything like the quantity with which you find yourself.

If possible keep main stock of meats on the base of the freezer with a few selected chops and steaks in easily accessible baskets.
Mince, steak and kidney and *diced beef* are all available in 1 lb bags.
Meat products: a large and ever increasing range of meat products is available for home freezers.
Pork sausages, both skinned and skinless, are available in chipolata, standard and king sizes, and some beef sausages can also be purchased.
Beefburgers represent a considerable saving when bought in boxes containing twenty-four, and can be used very effectively to produce a quick tasty meal.
Pâté, both the smooth pâté de foie and the coarser country pâté are available, as are the more

expensive game pâtés, sold in 4 oz, 8 oz and sometimes 1 lb packs.

Prepared main dishes on the market range from delicious minced beef and gravy, faggots and gravy and shepherd's pie, to the more exotic Beef Strogonoff, Duck à l'Orange, Lobster Thermidor. These mostly come as 'boil-in-bag' preparations needing virtually no skill or time and only a pan of hot water and a source of heat to have an almost gourmet type meal on the table in 15–20 minutes. They are expensive because all the work has been done for you, but they are an effortless way of having a dinner party.

The first two items mentioned are also very useful to have in the freezer and can be used to produce lots of interesting dishes.

Pastry and Pastry Products: both shortcrust and puff pastry can be bought in 7½ oz, 13½ oz, and 3 lb blocks. Vol-au-vent cases in three sizes can be bought prepared ready to bake. Also available are the ready to bake sausage rolls, meat, poultry and fruit pies or puddings, and specially prepared pastry for Danish pastries.

Cakes: delicious Danish pastries imported from famous bakeries in Denmark may be just thawed and eaten with great relish. Small fancy cakes and the dairy cream cakes are all useful products to have in the freezer for unexpected guests.

Fish and Shellfish: almost every fish in every form can be bought for freezer storage: cod, plaice, haddock, sole, trout, salmon, *etc*, some smoked, some plain, some breadcrumbed, some battered and ready prepared dishes from fish cakes to Sole à la Bonne Femme! Shellfish including lobster, crab, scallops, prawns, shrimps, *etc*, can now be on the menu at home at a price much more realistic than the retail cost, and without awaiting the season for the product to be available fresh. Kippers with their many uses are a must in every freezer.

Poultry and Game: chickens, whole or jointed, roasting or boiling, cooked or uncooked, are all available from frozen food distributors and represent a real saving in time and money. Battered drumsticks, and boned and rolled cooked breast of chicken roll make good party fare.

Turkeys both large and small may be bought and stored for both Christmas and other times in the year.

Duck is available whole or halved, uncooked or cooked, even cooked with a wine sauce requiring nothing more than reheating. Game can be enjoyed throughout the year too, with pheasant, guinea fowl, etc available.

Pet Foods: raw and cooked meat packs for dogs can be bought at very economical prices.

Meat, Poultry & Game

All meat freezes well, and to have meat readily available is one of the outstanding advantages of freezer ownership, for it gives variety to menu planning, reduces shopping time and gives perhaps the greatest saving of money if purchased in bulk (see page 14).

Selection: Although it is sometimes said that freezing has a tenderizing effect on meat do *not* think that tough meat can be made more tender and acceptable by freezing! The rule must be that if finest quality meat is to come out of the freezer the best quality must be frozen.

What to look for in butchery terms

Confirmation —describes the shape of the animal, its attractiveness, roundness, plumpness if you like.

Finish—describes the distribution of fat, which should be uniform throughout the carcass, with no recognizable difference between fore and hind quarters.

Quality —describes the colour of the flesh (a good red colour) and the fat (not yellowing) and covers the marbling effect of the fat in the flesh. This often depends on the breed of animal, when one would look for a good age/weight relationship.

Condition—describes the time between slaughter and butchering, the aging or hanging of meat

to obtain the maximum flavour and tenderness. The above terms may perhaps help you to talk to and understand your butcher, meat wholesaler or farmer, when negotiating the purchase of meat for your freezer, but the best advice is to go to a reliable source and trust in the experience of the professional.

The butchering of meat: Only you will be able to decide whether you are:

(a) man enough physically to cut up a carcass of meat (b) whether you can stand psychologically to be surrounded with so much raw flesh (this is a lot if you are thinking in terms of half a cow) (c) whether you have the time to spend doing the butchering *and* the packing for your freezer, and, last but perhaps most important, (d) whether you have the skill to carry out the operation successfully.

Skilled butchery is a joy to see, and if you have no previous knowledge of this, join a class at your local education centre or ask for private lessons from your butcher! There is tremendous satisfaction in buying a whole or half carcass and doing everything yourself, and only after your first attempt will you decide that either you enjoy doing it and of course save money by so doing, or you may, for the first time, realize the skill of your butcher and decide 'every man to his trade!'

For those determined to have a go it is as well to start with half an English lamb, then graduate to a pig, and only to the hind and fore quarters of beef when you feel able to cope.

Essential equipment

A good strong sharp steel knife, plus an oiled stone (bought from an ironmonger). The flat edge of the knife is slowly rotated on the stone to give a good sharp edge. One should always aim to keep all knives as sharp as possible.

A tapered boning knife is also useful. It is surprising how much more meat can be removed from the bone with the right tool for the job.

A small knife, about the size of a vegetable knife, is useful to remove small pieces of fat, sinuses and gristle.

A saw is absolutely essential; buy a blade for your husband's hacksaw and keep it just for butchering purposes. A saw will present a good cut surface to the meat and avoid the splintering which often happens with a cleaver in inexperienced hands.

The cleaver is a very useful tool in skilled hands, but the operation needs to be completed with one fell swoop to give a clean surface.

Boning of meat: This has many advantages. Boneless cuts of meat take up as much as 25% less freezer storage space. It is easier to make meat neater and more compact without protruding bones that may puncture the packaging material. Having said the above I still have a fondness for good old fashioned meat on the bone and there is no truer saying than 'the nearer the bone the sweeter the meat'. Boning and rolling does, of course, make the joint easier to carve, and the bones can always be simmered to make stock, which should be reduced to good concentration and frozen.

GENERAL POINTS FOR MEAT FREEZING

Drip: The quicker the freezing the less 'drip' from the meat on thawing and unless the resultant drip is used in sauces or gravy it means that much of the flavour is thrown away, and quality and texture impaired. All attempts therefore to reduce the drip should be made; some meat is more prone to drip than others, beef and white poultry meat are worst sufferers, and pork and dark poultry meat suffer the least. Drip is least evident when correct aging, few cut surfaces, low storage temperature and slow thawing conditions are met.

Browning of lean: Sometimes meat seen in the freezer looks brownish and dull compared with the bright red of fresh meat, and this is due to oxidation caused by contact with air. Browning is most likely to occur with slow freezing and commercial air-blast freezing, and is more likely in salted meat since the salt affects the enzyme action. If meat is exposed to bright lights (in retail frozen food cabinets, for example), it is more likely to brown too.

Rancidity of fat: The fat of meat is the first affected when correct rules for freezing are not observed. Rancidity is accelerated by *light* and *salt* and the proportion of the fat meat. Thus beef and veal are least affected by rancidity and bacon is affected most of all.

Storage times: All the above points will help you to understand the differing storage times for various meats. The times recommended, when the quality, flavour, texture, *etc*, equal fresh, are as follows: beef: 8 months; lamb, pork and veal: 6 months.

It should be stressed that these should be taken as a guide, no serious health hazard will develop from eating meat weeks or even months over the recommended times, *but* the quality, flavour, texture, *etc,* will gradually deteriorate. It is recommended, too, that chops and steaks cut from the above animals should have a somewhat shorter freezer life than the larger joints, so if possible keep these well within the times shown above. Much lower down the keeping scale are the meat products for which the following serves as a guide: green bacon, unseasoned sausages: up to 4 months; offal (livers, kidneys, hearts, *etc*): up to 3 months; mince, cooked meats: up to 2 months; smoked bacon, seasoned sausages: 4 to 6 weeks.

Preparation and packaging of meat for the freezer

(a) Set the quick-freeze setting on your freezer to its lowest setting twenty-four hours before loading with the meat. Have as empty a refrigerator as possible (also set at coldest temperature) to chill the meat before freezing.

(b) Decide how the meat is to be butchered (joints, chops, *etc*) before it is even delivered, so that the cutting can be started promptly with as little delay in getting the meat into the freezer as possible. It is helpful to have a second pair of hands available, for encouragement, and to hold on to the carcass during the initial dissection, also to be packing for the freezer as the joints and chops, *etc*, are being cut.

(c) The kitchen must be cleared to give as much working surface as possible, and be scrupulously clean. All cutting tools must be ready sharpened, and a good supply of the right packing material available.

(d) Having cut the desired chops, *etc,* trim off any surplus fat, gristle or small sharp bones. Protect protruding bones with a pad of foil before wrapping in freezer paper, aluminium foil or polythene, and if in any doubt as to the effectiveness of your chosen wrapping overwrap with mutton cloth or an old stocking. The packaging must be really effective moisture vapour resistant material and as much air as possible must be excluded from the package before sealing with appropriate tape or ties. Don't make the mistake of packing several chops or steaks into one bag without a piece of paper or polythene or foil to separate each chop or at least pair of chops, or they will freeze together into the joint that has just been painstakingly cut! A double fold of separating material between each one will enable the chops to be removed singly and the pack returned to the freezer.

(e) Stewing and braising meats should be cubed and packed in 1 lb bags so that recipe amounts can be easily calculated.

Important freezing note

Remember that only 10% of *the total capacity of the freezer should be frozen at one time*. For example, with a 10 cu ft freezer (at 20 lb per cubic foot) only 20 lb of fresh meat should be placed in the freezer in any 24 hours. It will be seen from the quoted weights of the various carcasses that half a lamb could be frozen at one time, but half a pig may need to be done over two days, and beef may need three or four days. It is important not to overload your freezer with more than the recommended 10% or, not only will the quality of the meat suffer from slower freezing, but all other products in the freezer will suffer from the fluctuation in temperature caused by overloading with relatively warm fresh meat. Have you room in your refrigerator to store the meat to be frozen tomorrow and maybe the next day? If the answer is 'no', think carefully about the quantity you are buying and consider buying meat already butchered and frozen, only requiring storage in your freezer.

Thawing and cooking of meat from the freezer

Where it is recommended, or convenient, for meat to be thawed before cooking, the approximate thawing times are:

	Refrigerator	Room temperature
Joints over 3 lb	4–7 hr per lb	2–3 hr per lb
Joints under 3 lb	3–4 ,, ,, ,,	1–2 ,, ,, ,,
1 inch thick steaks in chops	5–6 ,, ,, ,,	2–4 ,, ,, ,,

Slow thawing in a refrigerator is strongly recommended, and cooking times and temperatures are then as for unfrozen meat.

Cooking from frozen

Roasting
Both large joints and individual small cuts can be safely roasted from the frozen state. Indeed many cuts of beef and lamb have a better flavour cooked frozen than when allowed to thaw before cooking. Pork, which must be thoroughly cooked, requires extended roasting to ensure even cooking throughout. With large pork joints, therefore, thawing before cooking is strongly recommended. When cooking from the frozen state, adjustments must be made to the oven temperatures and cooking times to guarantee complete success, and it is advisable to use a meat thermometer to check that joints are cooked through to the centre.

Recommended roasting times at Gas No. 4 or 350°F for frozen joints.

Small joints under 4 lb
Beef — 30 min per lb and 30 min over
Lamb — 35 min per lb and 30 min over
Pork — 40 min per lb and 30 min over
For joints over 4 lb add 5 minutes to *all* above times.

Pot-roasting
Cook from frozen. Seal all cut surfaces in hot fat to prevent excessive loss of juices.

Boiling
Thaw before cooking. Boiling from frozen can result in weight loss and poor flavour.

Stewing
Cook from frozen.

Grilling and Frying
Cook from frozen from low heat to high heat.

Note

Meat should not be stuffed before freezing, as storage life is considerably reduced.

SPECIAL POINTS ON DIFFERENT MEATS

Beef
No particular time of year is better than another for the slaughter of beef cattle. Age when slaughtered is between 15 months and 2½ years. The carcass should be hung under chilled conditions for 7–10 days prior to butchering and freezing. Overhanging should be avoided as it causes early rancidity. To indicate good age/weight relationship, the hind quarter should weigh 115–160 lb, fore quarter should weigh 100–130 lb. It is worth boning beef as most joints are large, and bone takes up valuable freezer space.

Joints: Decide on size of joints most suitable to your family's requirements and cut accordingly, remembering of course that meat from a larger joint tastes much better. Slices of cooked roast beef may be covered with gravy and frozen.

Steaks: Cut to preferred thickness.

Stewing Meat: Trim off fat and cut into cubes, and pack in known useful weights, *i.e.* ½ lb, 1 lb, 2 lb.

Mince: Trim off fat, mince and pack as above. May be formed into patties, balls and beefburgers, remembering flat portions will be more economical on freezer space. Do not season.

Lamb
New Zealand lamb is available throughout the year. English lamb is seasonal and is best bought for freezing during the spring and summer, when there is no need to hang or condition the meat and it may be frozen soon after slaughter. If purchased during the autumn or winter when older and fatter it needs to be conditioned (hung) for 7 days. Lamb is usually sold as whole or half side and each side would weigh between 15–20 lb for good quality lamb. Beware of sides much heavier as this indicates older meat. May be boned, but not so necessary from the point of view of storage space, but it is necessary to give additional protection to protruding bones so as not to pierce wrapping and possibly damage other packets in the freezer. May also be skinned before packaging if preferred.

Joints: Again decide on joints most suitable to your personal requirements. The leg and shoulder joints may be left whole or divided into two smaller joints of shank and fillet. If a whole lamb is purchased perhaps the leg and shoulder from one side should be left large, the joints of the other side divided.

Chops: The loin and the best end of neck may be frozen whole as joints (boned or unboned) or cut into chops and cutlets. Your normal meat shopping will tell you which will be more useful to you.

Stewing Meat: The neck and middle neck of lamb are normally used in casseroles and stews. It is worth cutting the neck through the spine into easily packable portions. It is not worth the time or the effort to bone the raw meat as it is so much easier to remove the bones after cooking.

Breast of Lamb: Depending on whether this is a popular joint with your family, you will decide whether to take off the breast wide or narrow. I personally feel it is well worth stuffing and roasting a breast of lamb. If time permits bone the breast and freeze without stuffing. The breast may also be chopped and used for stewing.

Pork

Pork is available throughout the year and it is usually recommended that it should *not* be hung if to be packaged for the freezer, because of the comparatively high fat content which oxidizes with long hanging and becomes rancid more quickly. Pork is usually sold as a side, and should weigh between 40–50 lb. Again the decision to bone is left to the individual.

Joints: You may like to keep a leg of pork whole and freeze it for Christmas. The hand of pork you may like to bone as it is an awkward joint to carve when cooked. It is a good joint to stuff in pocket made by removal of shoulder blade bone. The loin, with or without the kidney, may be frozen as a joint (boned or unboned).

Chops: If the ribs are chined, this means that when cutting the meat into chops you are able to decide firstly the thickness of the chop yourself and secondly have them all of uniform thickness. If the pork (and the same applies to lamb) is not chined, one simply follows through the line of each rib with a sharp knife and saws through each piece of spine bone at the junction with the rib. The loin, as in the lamb, may be cut into chops, leaving the kidney sliced in each chop or removed and packed separately.

Belly Pork: May either be packed as a joint (or two small joints), or cut into rashers for grilling or frying. This is a particularly good cut of meat and its potential much underestimated.

Fillet: Just like the fillet of beef, so there is this delectable piece of meat nestling inside the loin, sometimes known as the tenderloin. It can be frozen whole or sliced for subsequent quick roasting, grilling or frying.

Crackling: Pork just isn't pork without its delicious crisp crackling which remains just as good after freezer storage. I find it easier to score the skin soon after removing the pork from the freezer for thawing, whilst it is still quite firm. It is then possible to cut fairly narrow slits instead of the wide ones which are sometimes all that one is able to do with an unfrozen somewhat flabby joint.

Bacon

Because bacon is a cured meat and because of its relatively high fat content it does not keep as well as fresh meat over long periods of time, but is quite satisfactory over short periods.

Select—Tell your supplier you wish to freeze the rashers or joints and endeavour to purchase it on the day he receives it fresh from the wholesaler.

Preparation—Vacuum-packed rashers are best for freezing (make sure it is a vacuum-pack, not just a polythene wrapping). Check that there is no hole in the packaging, overwrap in foil and freeze. Fresh bacon joints should be cut to size suitable to your particular requirements (boned if possible), closely wrapped in foil and then in polythene bags.

Storage Life—Fresh bacon joints unsmoked—up to 8 weeks; fresh bacon joints smoked—up to 5 weeks; vacuum-packed joints and rashers—up to 10 weeks.

Thaw—Remove home-packed bacon from wrapping to thaw, leave vacuum-packs in wrapping to thaw. Completely thaw both before cooking.

If bacon joint appears to have a surface of salt when defrosted, cover with cold water, bring to boil, then drain and cover again with fresh cold water, bring to the boil, then simmer for 20 minutes to the lb, and 20 minutes over. For steaks or rashers cut from a thawed fresh bacon joint, dip each slice in bowl or hot water to remove surplus salt, dry with kitchen paper before grilling or frying.

Offal: kidneys, liver, hearts, sweetbreads, etc

Most important that this should be prepared and frozen quickly. Prepare as for cooking, coring kidneys, removing blood vessels, *etc.* Remove kidney from jacket of fat which will reduce the storage life of the kidney considerably because of the possible rancidity of the fat. Liver is best sliced before packaging. Wash all offal well and dry with clean cloth, then wrap, seal, label and freeze. Do not keep longer than recommended storage times (see page 17).

Prepared meats, sausages, meat balls, etc

Home-prepared meat balls and sausages should have little or no seasoning before freezing if storage for longer than about 4–6 weeks is desired. This, on the whole, defeats the object of freezing if one has to remove, thaw, season and reshape, *etc*, before cooking.

Cooked meat dishes

Underseason all stews, curries and casseroles as flavour is intensified during storage, and the keeping time is reduced for highly seasoned dishes. Better meal planning is achieved if meats (plainly cooked) are packaged in family sized portions and a selection of sauces (see page 90) are frozen separately. Thus the housewife is able to offer a wide selection of meals instead of being faced with say a large quantity of chicken and mushroom casserole when what she and her family feel like is a chicken curry! Tend to undercook rather than overcook, as dish will receive further cooking on reheating. Cooked meat dishes may be made from raw meat taken from the freezer, cooked and then frozen in their completed form. This may be considered to be the first time this meat has been frozen in its cooked state and not refreezing. I would hesitate, however, to return leftovers of this cooked dish to the freezer, for if nothing else, the quality of the food would suffer considerably. Aim to keep cooked meat dishes not more than 2 months.

Poultry and game

With frozen chickens, both portions and whole birds, available at such competitive prices it seems hardly worth the effort of home freezing battery chickens but if a source of free-range chickens can be found then perhaps one or two nice fat juicy chickens should be trimmed, trussed and frozen to be simply eaten as Roast Chicken. For those who declare that frozen chicken doesn't taste as chicken used to twenty years ago the answer is to try to replace some of the flavour that you may find lacking (see recipes page 48) but remember it is not the freezer that has affected the flavour but the mass production. As with everything produced in vast quantities, the flavour must be fairly bland to cater for the mass market.

Select—Young fleshy birds with a layering of fat underneath the skin, and with the skin untorn or blemished in any way.

Preparation—Pluck the chicken whilst warm, if necessary dipping the bird in hot water, but this should be done with care as too hot water or too long in it will damage the skin, especially of young birds, and increase the chance of freezer burn during storage. Singe small remaining feathers and hairs over a flame. Remove head and feet, and draw the entrails, separating the giblets, which should be frozen separately from the poultry if long storage life is desired. If several chickens are being prepared for freezing it is worth separating the livers for use in recipes on their own (see page 46). Place bird immediately in refrigerator to cool quickly.

Whole birds should be prepared as for cooking with legs and wings well trussed to the body to give compact shape. Place small pad of foil over any protruding bones so that they will not puncture the packaging. Wrap either in foil or gussetted polythene bag taking care to mould around the chicken excluding as much air as possible (see page 12). Seal, label with the type of bird, roaster, boiler, *etc,* and then freeze.

Important Note

It is not advisable to stuff poultry before freezing, because the stuffing itself takes a long time to reach the desired low temperature, thus giving possible food spoilage organisms the time and warm conditions necessary for their undesirable activity. The storage time in the freezer for stuffed poultry would be reduced to that of the stuffing (a little over a month) making unstuffed poultry a much more desirable freezer product.

Chicken Portions—Should be prepared like whole birds, but cut in portions suitable to your family's requirements. Poultry up to about 3 lb in weight should be cut into four, larger birds into more. Trim into neat even-sized portions, removing easily removable bones, protecting any others from damaging packing materials. Either pack separately, or pack together separating each portion with foil or greaseproof for easy removal when required.

Trimmings—Cook bones and trimmings in water to make broth, strain and freeze this stock for use in soups, sauces, and casseroles.

Cooked Chicken—Whole chickens and portions may be cooked and frozen on or off the bone, useful for advance preparation for parties and picnic meals.

Note

All the above information about chickens is also applicable to other poultry, *i.e.* ducks, geese, turkeys, *etc.*

Game
This is perhaps one case when freezing for out-of-season eating is definitely justified, so that the pleasures of delicious game pies, terrines and casseroles, *etc*, may be savoured during the remainder of the year.

Important rules for freezing: Bleed the bird as soon as possible, hang for times suited to your family's palate. Pluck, remove as much shot as possible, draw, wash well and drain. Wipe the surface of the bird with a damp cloth and pack in best quality polythene bag, excluding as much air as possible. Seal and chill in the refrigerator before freezing. To freeze cooked game, use recipes with sauce to cover, to prevent any moisture loss from the flesh.

Fish & Shellfish

Fish is one of the most successful and useful products of the freezer *but* freezing is best done by the commercial companies. It is essential that fish for freezing should be *fresh*; in fact, frozen not more than 24 hours after being caught.

However, just in case you live by the sea or a river, and have a fisherman husband here are the rules to be observed:

White fish
Select—only fresh fish, see above.

Preparation—fish should be prepared ready-to-cook when removed from the freezer. Scrape off the scales, using the back of a heavy knife. Make a slit down the body cavity from gills to vent, remove entrails and scrape the backbone clean. Remove fins, gills, head and tail, then wash the fish thoroughly inside and out.

Whole: Trim fins and tail if fish is small and is to be frozen whole. Do not freeze whole fish which are more than 2 inches thick. Prepare as for steaks.

Steaks: Fish steaks from 1 to 1½ inches thick are prepared by slicing the fish crosswise.

Fillets: One fillet is cut from each side of the fish. The skin may be removed from fillets if desired.

Freeze—Fish tends to dry out quickly in frozen storage, so protect it with the best moisture vapour proof containers and wrappings. Place double thicknesses of freezer paper between each fish, fillet or steak so they can be separated before completely thawed. Fish can be cooked in aluminium foil wrappings.

Freeze fish in meal-sized amounts. Label and date the contents of the package.

Crabs, lobster, salmon and trout
These may be the special treat fish that you may find yourself wanting to freeze for eating later in

the year. Fish, particularly shellfish, must be absolutely fresh and on the whole I would encourage you to eat these fresh when available and buy commercially frozen delectations from the sea from your frozen food supplier.

Crabs: Use only live crabs. Place in salted water, bring to boil and cook for 15 minutes to the pound. Remove all edible meat in the usual way. Keep white and dark meat separate if subsequent use of crab meat calls for one or the other. If crab is to be served with both meats mixed, this can be done prior to freezing, but do not season or spice until preparing for serving as the intensity of the seasoning will increase during freezer storage. Pack in best quality packaging to prevent any transfer of flavours. Work, pack and freeze as quickly as possible.

Lobster: As for Crabs.

Salmon: Sometimes useful to have whole salmon for a special party, but not more than 2 inches thick for good results; otherwise cut into steaks. Follow details given for preparing white fish.

Trout: Freshly caught trout may be cleaned (as for eating fresh) and frozen. Either pack individually in polythene bags or divide with separating paper and pack in one large polythene bag.

Storage times

White Fish: 3 months: to include plaice, sole, cod, haddock, *etc.*

Fat and Smoked Fish: 2 months: to include salmon, halibut, herrings, mackerel, trout.

Shellfish: 4 weeks: to include crab, lobster, crawfish, scampi, *etc.*

Thawing and cooking of fish

White Fish: Steaks, fillets and whole small fish may be cooked from frozen and are probably better for so doing. Allow a third to one half extra cooking time, graduating from low to high heat. If fish is to have egg and breadcrumb coating it must be allowed to thaw completely, as coating will not adhere to frozen fish. It could, of course, be coated before freezing and then it may be cooked from frozen. Frozen fish, if thawed, is cooked and timed just like fresh fish and should be used as quickly as possible.

Slow thawing in an unopened package in refrigerator is to be recommended, particularly for large fish, as less leakage and drip of natural juices occur with slow thawing.

Thawing times for solid 1 lb packs: up to 10 hours in refrigerator; up to 4 hours at room temperature. Do not accelerate under cold water.

Shellfish: Should be completely thawed for use in cocktails or salads. It is preferable for it to be thawed before using in cooked dishes, with perhaps free-flow prawns and coated scampi as the exceptions.

Thawing times per lb as above.

Vegetables & Herbs

VEGETABLES

Most vegetables, with the exception of salad ones which lose their crispness, will freeze; some freeze/thaw better than others; some are worth the freezer space, some are not.

As with fruit, it is vital not to be so intent on getting vegetables into the freezer that the pleasure of eating them fresh is denied. A trap many new freezer owners fall into during their first year is to freeze too many of one variety, and they are often found to be eating vegetables from the freezer when the following year's crop is fresh in the garden! Aim to freeze a variety of vegetables rather than 50 lb of runner beans for a family of two, so that you end up never wanting to see or eat a runner bean again however good they might be.

Unfortunately the fields thrown open to the public are often those rejected by the commercial companies because the vegetables are past their prime, or are either too large and old, or too tough to be worth freezing. As with fruit, it is wise to work out the time spent in gathering, blanching, packing, freezing, *etc,* and decide for yourself if it is worth it. Unlike fruits though, freezing is undoubtedly the best method of preserving vegetables and no canning or bottling, drying or salting can compare with the frozen product.

RULES FOR VEGETABLE FREEZING

1. Must be picked at their optimum point of maturity.
2. Aim to get straight from garden to the freezer in shortest possible time.
3. Gather vegetables if possible in the cool of the morning.
4. Keep cool to prevent wilting if delayed.
5. Wash, grade into uniform sizes (rejecting all but perfect ones) and trim as necessary.
6. Blanch in boiling water for correct time.
7. Cool in iced water (see page 22).
8. Drain, package in correct containers, seal and freeze.
9. Freeze in small amounts so that the above rules may be observed correctly without allowing a carelessness of timing to develop.
10. Freeze in portions suitable to family consumption.

Methods of freezing vegetables

Dry Pack: This is only satisfactory for the *short term* storage of vegetables in the freezer, but is nevertheless permitted, and useful, should time be of utmost importance, as perhaps, when the peas and beans are at their best the day before you are going on holiday! The flavour, colour and texture of these frozen vegetables noticeably deteriorates after periods of longer than 2–3 months and the unblanched vegetables should be eaten first. It is useful to have a pack of mixed diced vegetables for stews and casseroles which need not be blanched.

Water Blanching: Fresh vegetables contain chemical substances called enzymes which are essential for growth and ripening. The enzyme activity will continue at sub-zero temperatures, with consequent flavour, texture, colour and vitamin loss. The action of scalding in boiling water or steam will retard this activity. Enough boiling water must be used to ensure a rapid return to boiling point after the addition of the vegetables. One gallon of boiling water for 1 lb of prepared vegetables is recommended. It is essential, therefore, to have a large enough pan to hold the rapidly boiling water and a basket or sieve which will fit, to take the vegetables to be blanched. A special blanching basket is on the market, but a sieve or even a fine mesh chip basket works perfectly well. Once the water is boiling vigorously, immerse 1 lb of vegetables in the basket; the water should return to boiling point within 1 minute, and the timing of the blanching should start at that point. Times are given for each vegetable in the following pages. Immediately the recommended time is reached the vegetables in the basket should be plunged into cold water.

Worthwhile Tip: Ice is always recommended for keeping this cooling water as cold as possible. Freeze a plastic box full of water to give large solid block of ice; this will keep the water cool more effectively than small ice cubes and will not thaw or need replacing so often. The cooling should be accomplished as quickly as possible and the time taken to chill the vegetables should equal the blanching time.

Allow vegetables to drain, and pack as quickly as possible in polythene bags; remove as much air from the bags as possible, seal, label and freeze. The blanching water may be used up to 6 or 8 times.

Steam Blanching: The basic principles should be observed as for water blanching, but, using same large saucepan only 1 inch of water should be brought to boiling point and the basket of vegetables should be placed in the saucepan without touching the water. Cover with lid and again time blanching carefully, increasing the time by half as long again as water blanching, then proceed to cool, pack and freeze as above.

Complete Cooking: Sometimes it is desirable to completely cook the vegetable before freezing, *e.g.* vegetable purées, which are useful for baby food, cream soup, and special diets. Cook in boiling water until tender, mash, strain, or use electric blender, pack in small amounts for quick freezing and thawing, especially for use as baby food. Courgettes (baby marrows) may be cooked Provençal with tomatoes and garlic, and frozen completely cooked, as may a ratatouille (mixture of unusual vegetables), or even a cauliflower au gratin.

Thawing and cooking of frozen vegetables
Almost all frozen vegetables can be cooked from frozen and are better for this. The surest way of spoiling frozen vegetables, just as with fresh, is to *overcook*. It is therefore important to remember that in the blanching process partial cooking has taken place and must be allowed for in the final cooking time calculations.

If, as recommended, only young vegetables have been used for freezing then this too means reduced cooking time. This usually means that normal cooking time for fresh vegetables may be reduced by half.

Exception—Corn-on-the-cob, which must be thawed before cooking otherwise the corn would cook while the cob remained frozen.

Storage Life
Except where otherwise stated this should be taken as from 9–12 months.

Asparagus
Select—Young, tender stalks; discard those which are either limp or woody.
Preparation—Grade according to thickness of stalk, trim off tough end and any scales with sharp knife. Wash thoroughly and cut to even lengths.
Blanching Time

	Boiling water	Steam
Small stalks	2 minutes	3 minutes
Medium stalks	3 minutes	4½ minutes
Large stalks	4 minutes	6 minutes

Do not blanch in bundles or water will not penetrate to centre.
Freeze—Cool quickly, drain and pack neatly in appropriate quantities for use, or lay on plastic tray in freezer to firm, then package in polythene bags or plastic boxes. No headspace necessary. Seal and label.
Thaw—Just enough to separate for more even cooking.
Cook—Boiling water or steamer, 5–10 minutes depending on size; oven 45 minutes.
Use—With fish and meat dishes; in flans, soufflés, and chilled with salads.

Beans—runner and French
Select—Young, tender, preferably stringless beans.
Preparation—Top, tail and leave whole if small, otherwise cut or slice.
Blanching Time

	Boiling water	Steam
Whole beans	2–3 minutes	3–4 minutes
Cut beans	2 minutes	3 minutes
Sliced beans	1 minute	2 minutes

Freeze—Cool quickly, drain, pack in amounts suitable to your requirements in polythene bags or plastic boxes. Leave ½ inch headspace. Seal and label.
Thaw—Cook from frozen.
Cook—Boiling water or steamer, whole 7–8 minutes, sliced 5–6 minutes; oven 45 minutes.
Use—As hot vegetable, or chilled with dressing.

Broad beans
Select—Pods which are small and young; reject beans which appear starchy.
Preparation—Shell and grade for size.
Blanching Time—Boiling water, 2 minutes; steam, 3 minutes.
Blanch those of even size together.
Freeze—Cool quickly, drain and pack in quantities suitable to your requirements in polythene bags or plastic boxes. Leave ½ inch headspace. Seal and label.

Thaw—Cook from frozen.
Cook—Boiling water or steamer 8–10 minutes; oven 45 minutes.
Use—As fresh vegetable.

Broccoli

Select—Bright green (or good coloured purple or white) with tender stalks and compact heads; pick before buds fully open.
Preparation—Discard any woody parts or broccoli which is flabby and wilting. If necessary soak for 30 minutes in salted water to remove any insects. Wash thoroughly and slice into even sized pieces suitable for serving.
Blanching Time

	Boiling water	Steam
Thin stalks	3 minutes	4 minutes
Medium stalks	4 minutes	5 minutes
Thick stalks	5 minutes	6 minutes

Steam method is probably better as damage to heads is likely to be less.
Freeze—Cool quickly, drain well and pack in amounts suitable to your requirements in polythene bags or plastic boxes. Better packaging achieved if stalks and buds are packed in opposite directions giving more compact parcel. No headspace necessary. Seal and label.
Thaw—Just enough to separate for more even cooking.
Cook—Boiling water or steamer 5–8 minutes.
Use—As hot vegetable, with sauce as cauliflower cheese, or in made-up dishes.

Brussels sprouts

Select—Small, firm, sprouts of good green colour.
Preparation—Remove any loose outer leaves and the stem. Wash thoroughly, soaking in salt water if necessary. Grade for size, blanching even sized ones together.
Blanching Time—Blanching is definitely necessary for sprouts otherwise quality and short storage time make it uneconomical.
Small sprouts: boiling water 3 minutes
Medium sprouts: boiling water 4 minutes
Freezing—Cool quickly, drain and pack in amounts suitable to your requirements in polythene bags or plastic boxes. No headspace necessary. Seal and label.
Thaw—Cook from frozen.
Cook—Boiling water or steamer 5–8 minutes.
Use—As hot vegetable or deep fat fried in batter.

Cabbage

Select—Not really worth freezing as available throughout most of the year, and does not freeze well. Freeze only if no shortage of freezer space. Choose young crisp cabbage.
Preparation—Shred, cut into wedges, or separate leaves as desired.
Blanching Time—Boiling water for 1½ minutes.
Freeze—Cool quickly, drain and pack in amounts suitable to your requirements in polythene bags or plastic boxes. No headspace necessary. Seal and label.
Thaw—Cook from frozen.
Cook—Boiling water or steamer 5–8 minutes.
Use—Use only as hot vegetable; not suitable for use uncooked in salads such as coleslaw.

Carrots

Select—Only young carrots, the thinnings from the garden crop are best, to freeze whole.

Medium sized carrots are acceptable to freeze sliced for use in stews, casseroles, *etc.*
Preparation—Remove tops and tails, wash well. Should not be necessary to scrape young carrots. Scrape the medium sized ones and slice into rounds for stews.
Blanching Time—Whole carrots in boiling water for 4 minutes. Not necessary to blanch for use in stews, *etc.*
Freeze—Cool quickly, drain and pack in quantities suitable to your requirements in polythene bags or plastic boxes. Stew pack carrots may be packed all together as they will not adhere to each other and required amounts can be removed and package returned. Leave ½ inch headspace. Seal and label.
Even unblanched carrots keep 9–12 months.
Thaw—Cook from frozen.
Cook—Boiling water or steamer 5–8 minutes; oven 45 minutes.
Use—As hot vegetable.

Cauliflower

Select—White, clean and solidly formed head of cauliflower, bright green surrounding leaves will indicate freshness. Size does not matter at all but smallest should be broken into florets.
Preparation—Break cauliflower into even sized florets 1–2 inches in size. Wash and if necessary soak in salted water for 30 minutes to remove insects.
Blanching Time—Boiling water 3 minutes; steam 4½ minutes.
Small whole cauliflower not more than 4–5 inches in diameter should be blanched in boiling water for 5 minutes. A little lemon juice added to blanching water seems to keep florets firm.
Freeze—Cool quickly, drain and pack in amounts suitable to your requirements in polythene bags or plastic boxes; or lay on plastic tray open in freezer until firm, then pack. No headspace necessary. Seal and label.
Thaw—Cook from frozen.
Cook—Boiling water or steam for 8–10 minutes.
Use—As hot vegetable, with sauce for cauliflower cheese; as part of made-up dish.

Celery

Select—Not suitable for use as salad vegetable or when required uncooked. If available cheaply, young celery hearts are well worth freezing. Reject stringy celery. Small amounts useful for stew packs. See carrots.
Preparation—Wash, remove any grit and trim hearts to small compact shape, or cut sticks of celery to 1–2 inch pieces.
Blanching Time—Pieces in boiling water 3 minutes; hearts in boiling water 5 minutes. Not necessary to blanch for use in stews if stored for short periods only.
Freeze—Cool quickly, drain and pack in amounts suitable to your requirements in polythene bags or plastic boxes.
Stew pack celery pieces may be packed in bulk as they will not adhere to each other and required amounts can be removed and package returned to freezer. Leave ½ inch headspace. Seal and label.
Storage Life—9–12 months. Stew packs up to 3 months.

Thaw—Cook from frozen.
Cook—Hearts, boiling water or steamer 10–12 minutes; pieces, boiling water or steamer 5 minutes.
Use—In soups, stews, casseroles, *etc;* hearts served with cheese sauce.

Courgettes
Select—Baby marrows about 3–5 inches long and 1 inch in diameter. Large marrows are not worth freezing as water content is too great. Courgettes should be fresh and crisp when cut.
Preparation—Wash, do not peel, top and tail, and cut in half lengthways or slice in $\frac{1}{2}$ inch slices.
Blanching Time—Fried in butter for 1 minute or completely cooked Provençal, with garlic and tomatoes; boiling water for 1 minute; steam for $1\frac{1}{2}$ minutes.
Freeze—Cook quickly (butter fried and completely cooked ones are best cooled in refrigerator) and pack in polythene bags, plastic boxes or foil dishes depending on final cooking. Leave $\frac{1}{2}$ inch headspace. Seal and label.
Thaw—Cook from frozen.
Cook—Boiling water for 5 minutes, or fried in additional butter for 5 minutes.
Use—As hot vegetable, part of ratatouille Provençal, may be used to fill pastry case, sprinkled with Parmesan cheese.

Kohlrabi
Select—Small, young, tender kohlrabi.
Preparation—Trim off stalks and leaves, wash and peel thinly, slice in $\frac{1}{2}$ inch slices.
Blanching Time—Boiling water for 3 minutes.
Freeze—Cook quickly and pack in amounts suitable to your requirements in polythene bags or plastic boxes.
Thaw—Cook from frozen.
Cook—Boiling water 5–6 minutes.
Use—Serve as vegetable or with cheese sauce as vegetable main dish.

Leeks
Select—Young, clean leeks.
Preparation—Cut off excess green and root; easier to be sure of removal of grit if sliced.
Blanching Time—Boiling water for 1 minute.
Freeze—Cool quickly and pack in amounts suitable to your requirements in good quality containers to prevent odour transfer. No headspace necessary. Seal and label.
Thaw—Cook from frozen.
Cook—Boiling water 5–10 minutes.
Use—Soups, stews and casseroles.

Mushrooms
Select—Cultivated mushrooms are best. They should be very fresh, clean and white. Button mushrooms may be left whole, larger varieties sliced before freezing.
Preparation—Do not wash, only wipe with clean damp cloth. Trim end of stalk and slice larger mushrooms. A little lemon will help prevent discolouration. Either fry in butter 1–2 minutes (preferable method), or pack dry for short term storage, or steam
Blanching Time—Steam for $3\frac{1}{2}$ minutes.
Freeze—Cool quickly (buttered ones in refrigerator) and pack in suitable size polythene bags or plastic boxes. Leave $\frac{1}{2}$ inch headspace for blanched mushrooms. Seal and label.

Thaw—Fried, blanched and dry pack from frozen.
Cook—Fry in butter for 5 minutes.
Use—Fried with grills, *etc;* in stews, soups and casseroles.

Onions
Select—Crisp, firm, fresh onions, large for slicing and chopping, and small button.
Preparation—Peel, slice, chop, or leave button onions whole.
Blanching Time—Chopped onions pack unblanched; sliced onion rings, floured and blanched in oil for 1 minute; whole onions in boiling water 3 minutes.
Freeze—Cool quickly and pack all above in small quantities in good quality wrapping materials to prevent odour transfer. No headspace necessary. Seal and label.
Storage Life—Unblanched stew pack up to 3 months; fried onions 9–12 months.
Thaw—Cook from frozen.
Cook—Whole onions 5–10 minutes in boiling water; floured rings deep fat fry 2–3 minutes.
Use—Soups, stews, casseroles, sauces, made-up dishes containing onion freeze well; also use for French onion soup, onion sauce, *etc.*

Parsnips, turnips (swedes)
Select—The above vegetables when small, young, fresh, and only freeze if plenty of storage space in freezer.
Preparation—Remove tops, wash, peel and dice.
Blanching Time—Boiling water for 2 minutes, or not necessary for stew pack for short storage period, or completely cook and purée.
Freeze—Cool quickly and pack in amounts suitable to your requirements in polythene bags or plastic boxes.
Storage Life—9–12 months; 8–10 months as purée; up to 3 months for stew pack.
Thaw—Cook from frozen except for purée; allow to thaw unopened until soft; 2–3 hours at room temperature.
Cook—Boiling water 8–12 minutes; purée gently re-heated.
Use—In soups, stews and casseroles; or sieved for infant and invalid food.

Peas
Select—Young, fresh, sweet, tender peas with crisp, green shells.
Preparation—Pod, not necessary to wash.
Blanching time

	Boiling water	Steam
Small peas	1 minute	$1\frac{1}{2}$ minutes
Medium peas	$1\frac{1}{2}$ minutes	2 minutes

Freeze—Cook quickly, drain and pack in quantities suitable to your requirements. Leave $\frac{1}{2}$ inch headspace. Seal and label.
Thaw—Cook from frozen.
Cook—Boiling water or steamer 5–8 minutes; oven 45 minutes.
Use—As hot vegetable, for addition to mixed vegetables, soups, casseroles, *etc;* or served chilled with dressing.

Potatoes
Select—*Boiled:* Small, new, even sized potatoes; freeze only if direct from grower and plenty of freezer space available.
Chips: An excellent product to come from the freezer but simply not worth all the trouble of

preparation when commercially prepared ones are available.

Roast: Worth doing extra when roasting potatoes anyway.

Duchesse: Worth piping a few for parties.

Croquettes: Like chipped potatoes, buy commercial.

Jacket potatoes: Not as good as freshly baked, but useful for party preparation if they have been prepared with filling (cheese, sardine, *etc*); otherwise they may just as well be prepared fresh as no saving in time or effort.

Crisps, plain boiled, creamed potatoes: Not worthwhile!

Preparation—All as for fresh, all above cooked before freezing.

Blanching Time—None.

Freeze—Cool quickly under draught of cold air or in refrigerator. Freeze all uncovered for short time in the freezer until firm. As all are now individually frozen, each kind may be packed in large bag or box. Do not egg Duchesse potatoes before freezing, and wrap jacket potatoes individually in foil. No headspace necessary. Seal and label.

Storage Life—Up to 6 months.

Thaw—It is usually better to thaw for better judgement of reheating times. Small new potatoes and chips may be used from frozen.

Roast potatoes: Best thawed 1½ hours at room temperature.

Duchesse potatoes: Egg glaze whilst still frozen to avoid smearing shape, thaw ½ hour at room temperature.

Croquette potatoes: May be cooked from frozen; avoid too hot a fat for frying.

Jacket potatoes: Cook from frozen in slow oven.

Cook—*New potatoes:* Boiling water or butter 5–10 minutes.

Roast potatoes: May be reheated in hot oven, but best results when deep fat fried.

Duchesse potatoes: heat through and brown in very hot oven for only few minutes.

Croquettes: Deep fat fry until hot and even golden colour.

Jacket potatoes: Still wrapped in foil in slow oven 1–2 hours.

Use—As above.

Spinach

Select—Young, fresh, crisp and tender leaves of good green colour, without heavy midribs.

Preparation—Wash very thoroughly, cut off stems; may be cooked and sieved before freezing.

Blanching Time—Blanch only small quantities at one time to ensure heat penetration; boiling water for 2 minutes.

Freeze—Cool quickly, drain and package in quantities suitable for your requirements in polythene bags or plastic boxes. Leave ½ inch headspace. Seal and label.

Thaw—Just enough to separate leaf for more even cooking.

Cook—In very little boiling water, or steamer, or butter, 6–8 minutes.

Use—As cooked vegetable, sieved for basis of cooked dishes, Florentine, soufflés, *etc*; also infant and invalid food.

Sweet corn

Select—On-the-cob must be uniformly matured; pick when kernels are well rounded and milk is thin and sweet not starchy. Not really worth time and effort to remove from cob, use commercially frozen free-flow packs.

Preparation—Remove husk, silk, wash and grade for size.

Blanching Time—Blanch similar sized cobs together; small cobs in boiling water 5 minutes; medium cobs in boiling water 6½ minutes; large cobs in boiling water 8 minutes.

Freeze—Cool quickly, drain and pack singly or in pairs in polythene bags. No headspace necessary. Seal and label.

Thaw—*Must* be completely thawed before cooking (see page 22); approximately 3–4 hours at room temperature.

Cook—In boiling water 8–10 minutes; brushed with butter in oven 20 minutes.

Use—Whole as starters, also with Chicken Maryland.

Tomatoes

Select—Tomatoes are not the best vegetable for freezer storage, but they are worth freezing to use for cooking if available in the garden or if they are purchased *very* cheaply. Choose firm ripe tomatoes.

Preparation—Skin, slice or quarter and simmer in little water 5–10 minutes; make tomato purée—as above sieved; make tomato sauce—see page 92, recipe section; or should the greenhouse be full of just ripe tomatoes the day before you go on holiday, just wipe and place them all on plastic trays open in freezer to firm.

Blanching Time—None, or cook as above.

Freeze—In containers leaving 1 inch headspace if cooked. Use polythene bags for whole tomatoes.

Storage Life—Dry pack up to 3 months; cooked as above up to 6 months.

Thaw—Cook from frozen.

Cook—Too watery to fry for breakfast; heat through sauce, soups and purée slowly in lidded pan.

Use—In all cooked dishes where tomatoes are used, reduced liquid requirement for dish if whole (watery) tomatoes are used.

Mixed vegetables

Select—Young fresh vegetables which are appropriate when served together.

Stew pack: onions, celery, carrots, other roots.

Macedoine: peas, beans, diced carrots, corn off cob.

Preparation—*Stew pack:* prepare as for fresh, mixed together in appropriate quantities. Tie on bouquet garni (see Herbs, page 26) for complete convenience.

Macedoine: prepare according to individual directions, combine after blanching.

Blanching Time—Not necessary for stew packs; as appropriate for individual vegetables.

Storage Life—Stew pack up to 3 months; macedoine 9–12 months.

Thaw—Cook from frozen.

Cook—See individual vegetables to judge cooking time.

Use—Stews, soups, casseroles and where colourful vegetables are required.

HERBS

Although dried herbs have been with us for many years now herbs fresh from the garden may be stored in the freezer until their season is round again. Several different methods of freezing herbs all seem to work well. Try all of them with your favourite garden herbs and decide which method you think the best.

Parsley:

Method 1 Chop large quantity of fresh from the garden parsley (include some of the stalks for flavour), pack into plastic container and seal. Spoonfuls can be removed as required and the pack returned to freezer.

Method 2 Pick large bunch of fresh parsley (wash and dry carefully if necessary), gather all the stalks together and secure firmly, place bunch in polythene bag and freeze. For use, remove bunch of parsley, rub whilst still hard frozen on grater, return bunch to freezer. The compact bunch of parsley will chop itself when rubbed against the grater, but this method is only really successful if the freezer is in the kitchen. If it is further away the parsley bunch will have begun to thaw by the time you reach the kitchen and the grating will be less effective.

Method 3 For those with freezer away from the kitchen, parsley sprigs may be put into tiny polythene bags and frozen. These may then be removed individually and just rubbed between the palms of your hands as you return to the kitchen; the small packs of brittle crisp parsley will just crumble and may be removed from the bag ready chopped for use.

Mint: May be frozen as for Method 1 for parsley, or chopped and placed in ice-cube trays until almost full. Top up with a little cold water and freeze. When frozen remove from ice-cube trays and store in polythene bags or box, removing one or two cubes to add straight from the freezer to boiled potatoes or peas, or two or three cubes, allowed to thaw before adding vinegar or lemon juice for mint sauce.

Chives: Gather together a bunch of chives, trim to equal lengths and wrap securely to form a thick stick. Remove from freezer for use by slicing a few from the end with sharp knife or scissors and returning remainder to freezer storage. May also be chopped and frozen as Method 1 for parsley.

Bouquet Garni: Choose sprig of parsley (again include stalk), sprig of thyme and fresh bay leaf. Pack together in tiny polythene bags and freeze. Put quantity of bouquet garni packs in large bag or box or tie to packets of stew pack vegetables (see page 25).

Fruit

All fruit will freeze, some better than others, and careful consideration should be given to both the economics and the final use for the fruit before home freezing. Of course, if you have excess to your requirements in your garden then it is only sensible to freeze some for use later in the year, but once again I stress, do not neglect the pleasure derived from eating the fruit fresh. If you enjoy a day bent double picking fruit in the fields when they are thrown open to the public, then by all means pick for the freezer for out of season eating, but *do* work out the cost of the fruit, the cost of the packaging, the cost of petrol getting you to the fruit farm, the price you put on your own time in preparing the fruit for the freezer, and *then* and most important, compare the quality and cost with commercially frozen and fruit preserved by other methods.

RULES FOR FRUIT FREEZING
1. Must be of prime quality.
2. At optimum point of freshness.
3. No blemished fruit.
4. Carefully and quickly washed only if necessary.
5. Protected from air to minimize discolouration.
6. Galvanized iron, copper or chipped enamel utensils, which may taint and discolour fruit should not be used.

Methods of freezing fruit

Dry Pack: A satisfactory method for fruit which can be prepared without breaking, or with fruit that does not discolour during preparation. Lay fruit open on trays and freeze uncovered until firm (25–50 minutes depending on size of fruit) then pack, seal and freeze in large containers as contents will be free-flow and small quantities can be easily removed. This flash freeze method is useful for a few prime selected fruits which will be used for decoration. Fruit frozen by this method will have a slightly shorter storage life. For jam-making, store fruit in polythene bags until required.

Sugar Pack: This is the best method for soft juicy fruit. Wash and drain selected fruit for freezing, layer fruit and sugar alternately in chosen freezer container, seal, label with method used, and freeze. Alternatively, fruit may be gently tossed in large bowl until each piece is sugar coated, then packed, sealed, labelled and frozen. The amount of sugar (preferably caster) will depend on the tartness of the fruit; 1 lb of sugar to 3–5 lb of fruit should be used as a guide. Allow headspace in packaging.

Syrup Pack: This method should be chosen for fruits which discolour quickly during preparation and those which have little natural juice. The strength of the syrup used is determined by the sourness of the fruit and personal preference. Medium strength (40%) is suitable for most fruits and tastes, but a lighter, weaker solution (20–30%) should be used for delicate flavoured fruit.

Quantities for syrup strengths:

30% (light) syrup is made up with 2 cups sugar 4 cups water; 40% (medium) syrup is made up with 3 cups sugar 4 cups water; 50% (heavy) syrup is made up with 4 cups sugar 4 cups water.

Sugar may be dissolved in hot or cold water but *must* be chilled before being added to fruit. It is useful to have a store of syrup in the refrigerator during the fruit freezing season.

The amount of syrup to fruit is about ½ pint to 1 lb fruit and sufficient syrup to cover the fruit in the packaging should always be used, or discolouration will take place.

Either put the fruit straight into bowl of syrup then portion and pack, or pack fruit in freezer container and cover with syrup. Ensure fruit remains submerged under syrup protection by topping with piece of crumpled foil or wax paper before sealing container. Allow headspace in packaging.

Use of ascorbic acid: This will help to retard the browning of light coloured fruit which will usually be frozen in syrup. Ascorbic acid can be purchased from chemists. Dissolve a good pinch in the syrup for each 1 lb pack.

NOTES ON THE THAWING OF FRUIT

All fruits, except dry pack, should be thawed in *unopened* containers. The container should be turned over several times during defrosting to keep fruit continually covered by syrup and to ensure even thawing.

Most fruits like slow thawing and fruits to be eaten uncooked should be served chilled.

Unless otherwise stated thawing times for 1 lb packs may be taken as 6–8 hours in refrigerator, 2–4 hours at room temperature and ½–1 hour under cold water and storage life may be taken as up to 12 months.

Apples

Think twice before using valuable freezer space with apples which are available all the year round.

Preparation—Wash, peel, core and quickly slice. The use of salted water or lemon juice will help prevent discolouration.

The apples may be blanched (see vegetable section, page 22) in boiling water (1–3 minutes), or steam blanched (2–5 minutes), the time depending on the thickness of the slice, but take care not to over-cook.

Freeze—Dry pack; sugar pack using ½ lb sugar to 2 lb apples; syrup pack using 40% sugar solution.

Storage Life—Dry pack up to 10 months; sugar and syrup packs up to 12 months.

Thaw—Leave unopened, turning pack over during defrosting; for subsequent further cooking may be used when par-thawed enough to separate.

Use—Fruit pies, flans, crumbles, mousse, creams, etc; for apple-sauce cook to pulp without water, cool, pack in suitable sized containers leaving headspace, seal and freeze.

Apricots

Select—Firm, ripe, evenly coloured apricots.

Preparation—Wipe, do not peel, halve and stone. Prepare quickly or use ascorbic acid as they soon discolour; for each 2 lb fruit use ¼ teaspoon ascorbic acid to ½ pint cold water.

Freeze—Sugar pack using ½ lb to 2 lb apricots; syrup pack using 40% sugar solution.

Storage Life—Up to 12 months (only 6 months if stones not removed).

Thaw—In unopened container turning pack during defrosting.

Use—Fruit salads, flans, creams, mousse, etc.

Bilberries

This fruit stains containers badly so lining with polythene bag is advised.

Preparation—Wash and drain.

Freeze—Dry pack; syrup pack using 40% solution.

Thaw—In unopened container turning pack during defrosting; may be used when only par-thawed for subsequent further cooking in pies, crumbles, etc.

Thawing Times—(1 lb packs) 6–7 hours in refrigerator; 2–3 hours at room temperature; ½ to 1 hour under cold water.

Use—In pies, crumbles, flans, creams, mousse, etc.

Blackberries

Select—Firm, plump, fully ripe blackberries.

Preparation—Wash, drain (discard over or under ripe fruit).

Freeze—Dry pack (suitable for subsequent jam making and to provide a few special ones for decoration); sugar pack using ½ lb sugar to 2 lb blackberries; syrup pack using 40% solution.

Thaw—In unopened container turning pack during defrosting; may be used when only par-thawed if to be subsequently cooked in pies, etc.

Thawing Times—(1 lb packs) 6–7 hours in refrigerator; 2–3 hours at room temperature; ½ to 1 hour under cold water.

Use—In jam, jelly, pies, crumbles, etc.

Cherries

Preparation—Remove stalks, wash, drain and remove the stones which tend to flavour fruit during storage. Just a few selected cherries still on the stalk may be frozen for decorative purposes.

Freeze—Dry pack for small quantity as above; sugar pack using ½ lb sugar to 2 lb stoned cherries; syrup pack using 40% solution.

Storage Life—Dry pack up to 6 months; sugar and syrup up to 12 months.

Thaw—In unopened container turning pack during defrosting; may be used par-thawed when required for subsequent further cooking.

Use—In fruit salads, flans, pies, crumbles, etc.

Currants—black and red

Preparation—Top and tail currants, wash and drain.

Freeze—Dry pack (suitable for subsequent jam making); sugar pack using ½ lb sugar to 2 lb currants; syrup pack using 40% solution.

Storage Life—Dry pack up to 10 months; sugar and syrup up to 12 months.

Thaw—In unopened container turning pack during defrosting; may be used par-thawed when required for subsequent further cooking.

Use—In jam, jelly, pies, crumbles, etc.

Damsons

Not particularly successful as skins toughen and stones tend to flavour fruit.

Preparation—Either wash and dry whole fruit, or cook to purée removing stones and skin.

Freeze—Dry pack (suitable for subsequent jam

making) or purée in polythene containers leaving headspace.

Storage Life—Whole fruit only a matter of weeks; purée up to 6 months.

Thaw—In unopened container.

Use—Jam and jelly or damson cheese.

Gooseberries

Select—Ripe gooseberries.

Preparation—Top, tail, wash and drain.

Freeze—Sugar pack using ½ lb sugar to 2 lb gooseberries; syrup pack using 50% solution.

Thaw—In unopened container turning pack during defrosting; may be used par-thawed when required for subsequent further cooking.

Use—Pies, tarts, flans, creams, *etc*.

Grapefruit

Only worth freezing if available very cheap. Grapefruit shells may be frozen and stored for use as containers for sorbets, but should not be frozen whole as flavour of skin and pith penetrates the flesh.

Preparation—Divide into segments either from whole fruit after peeling, or cut in half with flesh removed as for fresh grapefruit; remove pith and pips.

Freeze—Syrup pack using 50% solution (adding juice from grapefruit to solution to reduce to 40% solution, if little juice in fruit use 40% solution).

Storage Life—2–3 months.

Thaw—In unopened container turning pack during defrosting.

Use—As fruit cocktail, with or without other fruits; serve chilled.

Grapes

Small seedless sultana grapes give best results.

Preparation—Remove from bunch, wash and dry.

Freeze—Dry pack (best method, will *not* stick together); syrup pack using 40% solution.

Storage Life—Dry pack up to 10 months; syrup pack up to 12 months.

Thaw—Dry pack may be used from frozen for addition to fresh fruit salad and cooked dishes; syrup pack in unopened container turning pack during defrosting.

Thawing Times—(1 lb packs) 6–7 hours in refrigerator; 2–3 hours at room temperature; ½–1 hour under cold water.

Use—In fruit salads, flans, creams, and as accompaniment to many fish dishes.

Lemons

Unless available very cheaply there is little point in freezing lemons which are available all the year round. However, the following points are worthy of mention:

(a) lemon shells may be used for the serving of fish pâtés.

(b) lemons from which the juice has been removed may be frozen for use when grated lemon is needed; best to grate straight from frozen.

(c) quantities of grated lemon may be frozen and will remain free-flow for the easy removal of small quantities.

(d) lemon slices may be frozen in ice cubes for use in drinks.

(e) lemon juice may be frozen in ice cubes and defrosted in saucepan for immediate use.

Melons

Not particularly successful for home freezing because of high water content, commercially prepared melon balls in syrup are quite acceptable. Freeze empty fresh melon shells for use filled with commercially frozen melon balls.

Preparation—Halve, de-seed, cut into slices, cubes or balls, of uniform size.

Freeze—Syrup pack using 30% solution; close wrap melon shell in polythene.

Storage Life—Up to 6 months.

Thaw—In unopened container turning pack during defrosting. Keep melon shell frozen until ready to serve.

Use—With grapefruit segments in Florida cocktail; with shells (prawns, crabmeat, *etc*) for starters; with fresh fruit as salad base; with sorbet ice as refreshing dessert.

Oranges

For orange segments see Grapefruit, although oranges may be frozen whole as flesh not affected as in grapefruit. For marmalade making Seville oranges may be frozen just stored in polythene bags until you have time for marmalade making later in the year. Freeze orange shells for use as sorbet containers. Freeze left-over orange rind for use in grating.

Greengages—See Plums.

Loganberries—See Blackberries.

Peaches

Select—Firm, fully ripe peaches.

Preparation—Skin (if possible without plunging into water, otherwise into boiling water for 30 seconds and then into cold); halve, remove the stone and slice if desired; use ascorbic acid to prevent discolouration.

Freeze—Sugar pack using 5 oz sugar to 2 lb stoned peaches; syrup pack using 50% solution.

Storage Life—Up to 10–12 months.

Thaw—In unopened container turning pack during defrosting.

Use—As dessert with cream or ice cream, in flans, trifles, *etc*.

Pears

Do not freeze well. Do not waste valuable freezer space on this fruit unless necessary.

Select—Choose strong flavoured, fully ripe pears.

Preparation—Peel and slice and cook in boiling 40% sugar syrup for 1–1½ minutes.

Freeze—Sugar syrup using 40% solution as above.

Thaw—Gently stew pears in the syrup either in oven or in heavy based pan on top of stove, allow to cool in refrigerator.

Thawing Times—Under cold water to release from packaging, then cook as above from frozen.

Use—With other fruit so that texture and flavour is more acceptable, or in made-up dishes like tarts, flans, *etc*.

Pineapple

Not really worth freezing as they are very rarely cheap in this country and the tinned variety is preferable.

Plums

If frozen whole (unstoned) the storage life is reduced to a few weeks, as stones tend to flavour fruit.

Preparation—Halve and stone.

Freeze—Syrup pack using 50% solution.

Thaw—In unopened container turning pack during defrosting, or use from frozen for dishes requiring cooked plums.

Use—In flans, crumbles, pies, *etc.*

Raspberries—See Blackberries.

Thaw—Do not accelerate thawing by cold water method.

Thawing Times—See Strawberries.

Note: raspberries are much more successful than strawberries.

Rhubarb

Select—Only young, tender, stalks should be used.

Preparation—Wash and cut into 1–3 inch lengths, blanch in boiling water for 1 minute, drain, dry and cool.

Freeze—Dry pack; syrup pack using 40% solution.

Storage Life—Dry pack up to 10 months; syrup pack up to 12 months.

Thaw—Dry pack may be thawed just sufficiently to separate for use in pies and crumbles; syrup pack in unopened container, turning pack during defrosting.

Use—In pies, tarts, crumbles, or stewed.

Strawberries

Although almost everyone's favourite fruit it is really not so successful in the freezer as one might hope. They usually result in a rather sloppy, watery fruit if care in the selection (variety) and thawing is not taken.

Preparation—Remove hulls and wash or wipe only if necessary; may also be sliced, mashed or puréed.

Freeze—Dry pack for specially selected prime fruit for decoration; sugar pack using ½ lb sugar to 2 lb strawberries; syrup pack using 50% solution.

Thaw—Experiment with strawberries for decoration to calculate thawing time for maximum quality/appearance. Note timing for both refrigerator and room temperature defrosting. In sugar and syrup pack thaw in unopened container turning pack during defrosting. Do *not* use cold water method.

Thawing Times—Single strawberries *could* be 20–30 minutes at room temperature; 35–45 minutes in refrigerator. Best to eat with a few ice crystals still remaining. For 1 lb packs, 5–7 hours in refrigerator; 2–3 hours at room temperature.

Use—Best used where appearance of strawberry is not of paramount importance as in pies, glazed flans, creams, mousses, trifles, *etc*, because of tendency of fruit to collapse in spite of all precautions.

Dairy Produce

Eggs, and sometimes butter and cheese, have a cheaper season when it is worth buying in bulk. It is always worth having a small amount of these products in the freezer for emergencies, but with the exception of cream most dairy produce has a reasonable refrigerator storage life so do not waste too much valuable freezer space storing unnecessarily.

Milk: Ordinary fresh milk does *not* freeze well and tends to separate. Homogenized milk freezes much better and it is worth having a small quantity in the freezer.

Freeze—Pack in plastic or waxed containers leaving 1 inch headspace or if purchased packed in waxed cartons place straight in freezer.

Storage Life—About 4 weeks.

Thaw—In refrigerator if possible, but may be accelerated if to be used in cooking.

Important Note: Do not freeze milk in milk bottle as expansion during freezer storage will cause bottle to crack.

Cream: The butterfat content of cream needs to be 35% or above, for successful freezing, therefore single cream with only 18% butterfat is *not* successful and will separate when thawed. Freeze only really fresh cream.

Freeze—Whipping cream with 40% butterfat freezes well; leave ½ inch headspace for expansion on freezing. A little sugar added to cream before freezing helps to overcome any tendency to separation.

Clotted cream freezes well.

Whipped cream may be piped into rosettes, frozen uncovered until firm, then packed in airtight containers and stored. Use straight from freezer to decorate flans and desserts.

Small amounts (1 or 2 tablespoons) are often called for in a recipe, so it is useful to freeze cream in ice cube trays, removing from cube container when frozen to store in plastic box or polythene bag. Amounts can then be removed as required; 1 ice cube usually equals 1 tablespoon, but measure the amount each section of your particular ice cube container holds and note on label.

Storage Life—3 months.

Thaw—Best allowed to thaw slowly in refrigerator for several hours.

Butter: Must be fresh.

Freeze—Commercial wrap is adequate for freezing but storage life lengthened if over-wrapped in polythene or foil.

Storage Life—Unsalted 9–12 months; salted 6 months.

Thaw—About 30 minutes (per ½ lb) at room temperature, but better if allowed to thaw more slowly (about 2 hours) in refrigerator.

Useful butter products worth freezing

1. Butter pats or balls in preparation for a party: freeze open on tray until firm; pack and store. Use straight from freezer.
2. Parsley or garlic butter: roll into cylinder; wrap in foil; slice from roll from frozen for steaks, chops, *etc*.
3. Hard sauces like Rum Butter: freeze in plastic containers, thaw in refrigerator for about 2 hours.
4. Butter spreads for sandwiches and canapés: freeze in small quantities, thaw in refrigerator.
5. Butter icings: may be piped as for fresh cream for instant cake decoration.
6. Roux for sauces: make up quantity using equal butter and flour, divide into 1 oz packs (½ oz butter, ½ oz flour) wrap in foil and freeze. To make white sauce drop 1 roux pack into ½ pint of milk and bring to boil, stirring until thick and smooth.

Margarine: May be frozen, with storage life of up to 12 months, but only worth it if purchased cheaply and plenty of freezer storage space available.

Lard: May be frozen, with a storage life up to 4 months but, as above, only worth the freezer space if bought cheaply or rendered when pork is being home butchered and prepared for the freezer.

Cheese: Hard cheese freezes well. The blue cheeses tend to be rather crumbly after freezer storage. Cream cheeses may become a little granular on thawing. Freeze all cheeses at desired maturity.
Freeze—Cut into portions suitable to requirements, wrap in good moisture vapour resistant material to prevent drying and flavour transfer.
Storage Life—Hard and blue cheeses 3 months; cottage cheese 2–3 months; cream cheese 1–2 months.
Thaw—All cheeses in refrigerator for several hours. To overcome granular texture in cream and cottage cheese add a little cream or top of milk before serving.

Grated cheese: A great asset to have always to hand in the freezer. Grate a large quantity, preferably in mill or electric shredder and pack in polythene box with well fitting lid. Use straight from frozen as required. It remains quite free-flow so it is not necessary to pack in small quantities.

Eggs: Fresh eggs in the shell cannot be frozen as shells would crack due to expansion of contents. Hard-boiled eggs are not successful frozen as the white becomes rubbery and unpalatable.
Freeze—Whole eggs (unbeaten) may be frozen individually in small foil containers. Whole eggs (beaten)—to each egg add either ¼ teaspoon of salt or 1 teaspoon sugar to maintain good texture. Yolks and whites (separately) as above.
Note
Label salt or sugar, and use in appropriate savoury or sweet dishes.
It makes assessment of quantities easier if the beaten eggs are frozen in ice cube containers, then separated and packed noting egg cube amount.

Storage Life—6–9 months.
Thaw—in refrigerator 3–4 hours; at room temperature 1½ hours; in container in warm water ½ hour. Individual whole frozen eggs may be poached either in or out of container, allowing a little extra cooking time.
Quantities: When beaten eggs are frozen in quantity it is as well to know these spoon measures as a guide:
Beaten whole egg—3 tablespoons = 1 egg
Beaten white —2 tablespoons = 1 egg
Beaten yolk —1 tablespoon = 1 egg
10 beaten whole eggs = 1 pint
24 beaten egg yolks = 1 pint

Ice cream: Perhaps not primarily considered to be a dairy product, but as it is made up of mainly dairy produce it seemed logical to include it in this section.
Home-made ice cream made in the freezer is more successful than made in ice box of domestic refrigerator as the freezing process is much quicker, preventing the large ice crystals which form with the slow freezing process.
Freeze—Pack in good quality moisture vapour proof containers, preferably in amounts suitable to your needs rather than in large containers. This will then prevent the fluctuations in temperature which are inevitable when removing small quantities from large containers. Too many variations in temperature cause poor texture.
Storage Life—3–4 months; the better the quality of the ingredients the longer the Ice cream will retain its flavour and texture.
Thaw—May be used straight from the freezer, especially if served with hot sauce, but flavour is usually better developed if allowed to thaw for just a short time in the refrigerator. Ice cream thaws more quickly in metal containers than plastic.

Breads, Cakes & Pastries

Most varieties of all three freeze well, and can be frozen prior to baking, par-baked, or completely cooked. All are handy for unexpected guests.

Yeast
Fresh yeast freezes well and the yeast cells are not destroyed by low temperatures. Yeast may

cream itself on thawing, but its activity is still all right.

Freeze—Weigh out into quantity normally used $\frac{1}{4}$ oz, $\frac{1}{2}$ oz, or 1 oz. Wrap each piece individually and pack into polythene box, labelled and dated.

Storage Life:—Up to 12 months.

Thaw—Allow 30 minutes at room temperature or grate coarsely straight from freezer.

Baked bread

All baked bread, bought or home-baked, freezes well, provided it is freshly baked when frozen. Storage time varies with the type of bread.

Freeze—Wrap in heavy duty aluminium foil or polythene bags. Commercially sliced loaves may be stored in own waxed paper wrapper.

Storage Life—White and brown bread keeps well for up to 4 weeks. Enriched bread and rolls (milk, fruit, malt loaves and soft rolls) keep up to 6 weeks. Crisp crusted loaves and rolls have a limited storage time as the crusts begin to shell off after 1 week. Vienna type loaves and rolls keep for 3 days only.

Thaw—Leave loaves in packaging at room temperature for 3–6 hours depending on size of loaf, or leave overnight in refrigerator, or place frozen loaf wrapped in foil in fairly hot oven, Gas No. 6 or 400°F (204°C) for 45 minutes.

Sliced bread can be toasted from frozen.

Place frozen rolls wrapped in foil in very hot oven Gas No. 8 or 450°F (232°C) for 15 minutes, or leave in packaging at room temperature for $1\frac{1}{2}$ hours.

Note

Crusty loaves and rolls thawed at room temperature should be refreshed before serving. Place unwrapped loaves or rolls in fairly hot oven Gas No. 6 or 400°F (204°C) for 5–10 minutes.

Bread doughs, risen and unrisen

Standard bread recipes can be frozen, with best results obtained from doughs made with 50% more yeast than in standard recipes, *i.e.* $\frac{1}{2}$ oz yeast should be increased to $\frac{3}{4}$ oz.

Freeze dough in quantities you are most likely to use: 1 lb 2 oz dough for 1 lb loaf tin.

Heavy duty polythene bags, lightly greased, are best. They must be tightly sealed as any air left inside causes skinning on the dough surface, which will crack during handling, and gives the baked dough crust a streaky appearance. If there is a chance of the dough rising a little before freezing leave 1 inch of space above the dough.

Storage Life—unrisen plain white and brown doughs keep up to 8 weeks; enriched dough keeps up to 5 weeks.

Risen plain and enriched white and brown doughs keep up to 3 weeks.

Part-baked rolls and loaves

Both home-baked white and wheatmeal rolls can be frozen partly baked. This is a very successful method as the frozen rolls can be put straight from the freezer into the oven to finish baking; ideal to serve for breakfast. Loaves are not so successful as rolls because during part-baking the crust becomes well-formed and coloured before the centre of the loaf is set.

Part-baked loaves and rolls available in shops freeze well.

To part-bake rolls—Place shaped and risen rolls in cool oven Gas No. 2 or 300°F (149°C) for about 20 minutes. The rolls must be set, but still pale in colour. Cool.

Freeze—Pack cooled rolls in usable quantities in heavy duty foil or polythene bags. Seal and freeze. Care must be taken when packing to avoid squashing.

Storage Life—Up to 4 months.

Thaw—Unwrap and place frozen rolls in oven to thaw and complete baking. Bake white rolls at Gas No. 6 or 400°F (204°C) brown rolls at Gas No. 8 or 450°F (232°C) for 20 minutes.

Bought part-baked rolls and loaves

Freeze—Freeze immediately after purchasing, ensuring that they are freshly delivered to retailer. Leave loaves in polythene bags they are sold in. Pack rolls in polythene bags and seal.

Storage Life—Up to 4 months.

Thaw—*Loaves:* place frozen unwrapped loaf in a hot oven, Gas No. 7 or 425°C (218°C) for 40 minutes. Cool for 1–2 hours before cutting.

Rolls: place frozen unwrapped rolls in a fairly hot oven Gas No. 6 or 400°F (204°C) for 15 minutes.

Sandwiches

White or brown sandwiches freeze well. All varieties can be frozen—closed, rolled, *e.g.* asparagus rolls and pinwheels, club, open, Neapolitan or ribbon sandwiches. Pack as individual sandwiches or in stacks of the same filling, interleaved with foil or polythene sheets.

Freeze—Wrap in heavy duty foil or polythene bags, label with type of filling, quantity and date.

Rolled sandwiches: pack asparagus rolls closely together on a tray to prevent them unrolling. Seal with heavy duty foil.

Pinwheels, club and ribbon sandwiches: freeze uncut wrapped tightly in foil.

Open sandwiches: freeze without salad garnishes in a single layer in a sealed polythene container.

Ordinary sandwiches: freeze with crusts on to keep moist. Use top and bottom crusts from loaf to give support to package.

Storage Life—Open sandwiches 1 week; all others up to 2 months.

Thaw—Leave in packaging. All sandwiches can be left overnight in a refrigerator or thawed at room temperature. Times vary depending on size of the package. Individually wrapped take 2 hours; stacks of 4–6 sandwiches 6–7 hours; rolled sandwiches 4–5 hours.

Pinwheels, club and ribbon sandwiches, which cut more easily when partially thawed take 3–4 hours; open sandwiches take 1–2 hours; garnish with salad before serving.

Toasted sandwiches: Place frozen unwrapped under a hot grill; they thaw whilst toasting.

Sandwich fillings: Meat, cheese and fish fillings mixed with butter or cream cheese freeze well. Fillings which are unsuitable for freezing are hard-boiled egg, which becomes rubbery, and high water content salad food such as lettuce, watercress, cucumber and tomato. Seasonings should be used sparingly, especially pepper and curry powder, as the flavour increases during storage.

Packed meals: Prepare a quantity of individual

31

frozen sandwiches, small pies and cakes for packed meals. Wrap individually in heavy duty foil or polythene bags for freezing. To thaw for lunchtime remove from freezer in morning, leave in wrapping and pack. Add fresh tomatoes, salad and fruit if wished.

Uses of bread
Breadcrumbs: Prepare fresh breadcrumbs in quantity for use in puddings, stuffings, sauces and coating fried foods. Frozen breadcrumbs remain separate and the required quantity can be easily removed.
Freeze—Pack in polythene bag, sealed polythene container or screw-topped jar.
Storage Life—Up to 3 months.
Thaw—Breadcrumbs need not be thawed for stuffings, puddings and sauces. To use for coatings, leave at room temperature for 30 minutes.
Fried Bread: Croûtons and fried bread shapes for canapés and party snacks freeze well and can be prepared in quantity. When frozen they remain separate and the required quantity can be easily removed.
Freeze—Pack in polythene bag, sealed polythene container or screw-topped jar.
Storage Life—Up to 1 month.
Thaw—Place frozen, uncovered, in fairly hot oven, Gas No. 6 or 400°F (204°C) for 5 minutes, or the tiny ones may be popped straight into hot soup.
Flavoured Breads: Garlic or other flavoured breads, which are delicious to serve with soups or at parties, can be frozen. Make 1 inch cuts along French or Vienna loaves to within ½ inch of the bottom. Spread creamed butter, flavoured with garlic, cheese or herbs, generously between slices.
Freeze—Wrap tightly in heavy duty foil.
Storage Life—Up to 1 week; the crust begins to shell off after this time.
Thaw—Place frozen, wrapped in foil, in fairly hot oven Gas No. 6 or 400°F (204°C). A French stick takes about 30 minutes to thaw and heat through; a Vienna loaf takes about 40 minutes.

Croissants and Danish pastries
Both baked croissants and Danish pastries freeze well. The unbaked dough can also be frozen in bulk, and may be stored for up to 6 weeks.
Baked croissants
Freeze—Pack in a single layer in a polythene bag or heavy duty foil, or place in a foil tray sealed with foil.
Storage Life—Up to 8 weeks.
Thaw—Place frozen, wrapped in foil in a moderate oven, Gas No. 4 or 350°F (177°C) for 15 minutes, or leave in packaging at room temperature for 1½–2 hours, then refresh, wrapped in foil, in a hot oven, Gas No. 7 or 425°F (218°C) for 5 minutes.
Baked Danish pastries
It is preferable to freeze the pastries without icing so that they can be refreshed in the oven, but they can be frozen when iced.
Freeze—Pack cooled pastries in a sealed polythene container or in heavy duty foil.
Storage Life—Up to 4 weeks.
Thaw—Iced pastries: Leave in loosened packag-

ing at room temperature for 1½ hours.
Plain pastries: As above, then refresh in a moderate oven Gas No. 4 or 350°F (177°C) for 5 minutes or place frozen in oven, at above temperature, for 10 minutes.

Savarins, babas, brioches and tea breads
For best results bake, then freeze.
Freeze—Wrap in heavy duty foil or polythene bags, then if decorated in boxes.
Storage Life—Savarins and Babas: Up to 3 months; *Brioches:* Up to 4 weeks; *Tea Breads:* Up to 6 weeks.
Thaw—Savarins leave in packaging at room temperature for 2–3 hours. Complete and serve. *Babas* place frozen, wrapped in foil, in a hot oven Gas No. 6 or 400°F (204°C) for 10–15 minutes, or leave in packaging for 45 minutes at room temperature; complete and serve.
Brioches place frozen, wrapped in foil, on baking tray in very hot oven, Gas No. 8 or 450°F (232°C) for 10 minutes.
Tea Breads leave in packaging at room temperature for 2–3 hours or, if undecorated, place foil-wrapped loaf in moderate oven, Gas No. 4 or 350°C (177°C) for 15–20 minutes.

Pizza
Freeze either unbaked or baked.
Unbaked:
Freeze—Prepare to baking stage; wrap in heavy duty foil or polythene.
Storage Life—Up to 3 months.
Thaw—Remove packaging and place frozen in cold oven set at Gas No. 8 or 450°F (232°C) turn on oven and bake for 30–35 minutes.
Baked:
Freeze—Wrap cooled pizza in heavy duty foil or polythene.
Storage Life—Up to 2 months.
Thaw—Remove packaging and place frozen in fairly hot oven Gas No. 6 or 400°F (204°C) for 20 minutes, or leave in packaging at room temperature for 2 hours before baking as above for 10–15 minutes.

Pastries
All pastries, unbaked or baked freeze well.
Shortcrust Pastry: Frozen in bulk takes 3 hours at room temperature to thaw before it can be rolled and there is little advantage in freezing it this way. Shape into pies, flan cases, tartlets or pie lids before freezing unbaked or baked.
Unbaked:
Freeze—Pies: make large pies in foil dishes or plates; make small pies in patty tins or foil dishes. Do not make steam vent in lid. Freeze uncovered. When frozen leave large and small pies in foil dishes, and seal with foil. Remove small pies from patty tins and pack in heavy duty foil or polythene bags.
Pie Lids: prepare in quantity and cut into shape to fit pie dish; freeze uncovered; pack several together separated by foil or polythene sheets in a box.
Flan Cases: freeze in flan ring or foil case until hard, remove ring or case, wrap in a polythene bag or heavy duty foil, then pack in a box for protection.
Tartlet Cases: Freeze uncovered in patty tins; when frozen remove from tins, pack in polythene or heavy duty foil. and pack in a box.

Storage Life—Up to 3 months.

Thaw—*Pies:* unwrap and place in a pre-heated oven and bake as usual, allowing extra time for thawing; cut a vent in the pastry when it begins to thaw.

Flan Cases: unpack and place frozen case into flan ring on a baking sheet; bake 'blind' at Gas No. 6 or 400°F (204°C) for 20–25 minutes.

Tartlet Cases—unpack and place frozen into patty tins and bake at Gas No. 6 or 400°F (204°C) for about 15 minutes.

Pie Lids: dampen edge of filled pie dish and place frozen lid on top, bake at Gas No. 6 or 400°F (204°C) for 20–25 minutes, reduce oven to Gas No. 2 or 300°F (149°C) and bake for a further 10–15 minutes.

Baked:

Freeze—*Pies:* bake in foil dishes or plates; cool quickly, leave in the dish and pack in heavy duty foil; freeze immediately.

Flan and Tartlet Cases: pack cooled cases in sealed polythene containers, in polythene bags or heavy duty foil, and then in a box.

Storage Life—Meat pie 3–4 months; fruit pies up to 6 months; unfilled cases up to 6 months.

Thaw—*Pies:* leave at room temperature for 2–4 hours depending on size of pie. Reheat in oven if required hot.

Flan and Tartlet Cases: leave at room temperature for about 1 hour.

Flaky and Puff Pastry
Unbaked:

Freeze—*Bulk Pastry:* prepare up to last rolling. Pack in polythene bags or heavy duty foil.

Pies: freeze as for shortcrust pastry pies.

Pie Lids: freeze as for shortcrust pastry.

Vol-au-vent Cases: prepare in quantity, freeze uncovered on a baking sheet or tray. When frozen, pack in sealed polythene containers, or wrap in polythene bags or heavy duty foil and pack in a box. Unless you enjoy making your own pastry buy commercially prepared pastry and vol-au-vent cases which are very good.

Storage Life—3–4 months.

Thaw—*Bulk Pastry:* leave 3–4 hours at room temperature or overnight in the refrigerator.

Pies: unwrap and place frozen in oven. Bake flaky pastry at Gas No. 7 or 425°F (218°C) for 25 minutes. Bake puff pastry at Gas No. 8 or 450°F (232°C) for 15–20 minutes. Reduce both oven temperatures to Gas No. 5 or 375°F (191°C) if filling requires longer.

Pie Lids: dampen edge of filled pie dish and place frozen lid on top. Bake as above for pies.

Vol-au-vent Cases: place frozen on a baking sheet in very hot oven at Gas No. 8 or 450°F (232°C) for 15 minutes.

Baked:

Freeze—*Pies* and *Vol-au-vent Cases:* can be frozen baked but are fragile to store and take up more room than when frozen unbaked. Pack carefully in sealed polythene containers.

Storage Life—Up to 6 months.

Thaw—*Pies:* leave at room temperature for 2–4 hours depending on size; reheat, if required. *Vol-au-vent Cases:* leave at room temperature for 1 hour or place frozen cases uncovered in very hot oven at Gas No. 8 or 450°F (232°C) for 5–10 minutes.

Choux Pastry
Savoury and sweet eclairs, profiteroles and cream buns can be frozen unbaked or baked.
Unbaked:

Freeze—Can be packed in bulk but is best when shaped before freezing as the frozen shapes can be baked while still frozen.

Bulk: place in a sealed polythene container.

Shaped: pipe or spoon pastry on to baking sheet and freeze uncovered. When frozen, remove from baking sheet and pack in polythene bags or heavy duty foil.

Storage Life—Up to 3 months.

Thaw—*Bulk:* leave at room temperature for 3–4 hours or overnight in the refrigerator.

Shaped: place frozen piped shapes on a greased baking sheet and bake at Gas No. 6 or 400°F (204°C) allowing 5 minutes longer than for freshly made pastry.

Baked:

Freeze—Split sides of eclairs and buns, and allow to dry out and cool quickly; pack in polythene bags or heavy duty foil.

Storage Life—Up to 6 months.

Thaw—Leave in packaging at room temperature for about 1 hour, then remove wrapping and refresh in a moderate oven Gas No. 4 or 350°F (177°C) for 5 minutes, or unwrap and place frozen into a moderate oven for 10 minutes. Cool, fill and decorate.

Suet Pastry
As suet pastry is quick and easy to make no advantage is gained from freezing it in bulk. Savoury or sweet puddings can be frozen uncooked or cooked and then placed straight from the freezer into the steamer. Uncooked puddings of the steak and kidney type require cooking time of about 5 hours and so are best frozen cooked. Remember not to overseason the savoury fillings.

Freeze—Make up cooked puddings in foil, or polythene basins, and cook; cool quickly, wrap basins tightly in foil and freeze.

Storage Life—Up to 1 month for meat puddings; up to 3 months for fruit puddings.

Thaw—Remove wrapping and cover top with foil or polythene lid and place, still frozen, in steamer; 1½ pint size steak and kidney pudding takes 3 hours and a fruit pudding 2½ hours; less in a pressure cooker.

Note
Alternatively, cooked fillings, especially meat, can be frozen separately and used with freshly made suet pastry when required.

Scones, cakes and biscuits
Baked Cakes and Scones: Scones and all types of baked cakes, plain or rich, freeze well. Swiss rolls, sponge cakes and flan cases, which do not keep long after baking, freeze extremely well. Cakes can be frozen undecorated or decorated (see note on icings). As rich fruit cakes keep well in airtight tins there is no point in freezing them.

Freeze—*Scones and Undecorated Cakes:* wrap cooled scones and cakes well in foil or polythene bags.

Decorated Cakes: freeze unwrapped to prevent damage to decoration. When frozen wrap well in foil. As baked cakes can be easily damaged after freezing place in boxes for protection.

Storage Life—Undecorated Cakes: up to 6 months. *Decorated Cakes:* up to 3 months.

Thaw—Scones: leave in packaging at room temperature for 1–1½ hours or place frozen, wrapped in foil, in a fairly hot oven, Gas No. 6 or 400°F (204°C) for 10 minutes.

Undecorated Cakes: leave in packaging at room temperature; small cakes take 1 hour, larger cakes 2–3 hours, sponge cakes and flans 1½–2 hours, Swiss roll 2–2½ hours.

Decorated Cakes: unwrap to prevent wrapping sticking to cake during thawing and leave at room temperature for 2–4 hours depending on size.

Unbaked Cake Mixtures: Rich creamed mixtures, *e.g.* for a Victoria sandwich, freeze satisfactorily. Whisked sponge cake mixtures do not freeze well.

Freeze—Freeze creamed mixtures in sealed polythene containers or cartons in usable quantities, or line cake tin with greased foil, add cake mixture and freeze uncovered. When frozen remove from tin, wrap in heavy duty foil and seal tightly.

Storage Life—Up to 2 months.

Thaw—Leave mixture in cartons at room temperature for 2–3 hours, then fill tins and bake. Return mixture frozen in tin shape to original tin and place frozen and uncovered in a pre-heated oven. Bake as usual allowing about 5 minutes extra for a sandwich cake, longer for deeper cakes.

Icings and Fillings: which freeze well are butter cream, fresh whipped cream, glacé icing, almond paste, jam glazes. Boiled icing, *e.g.* American frosting, soft meringue icing and custard filling do not freeze satisfactorily.

Unbaked Biscuit Mixtures: Any biscuit mixture containing over ¼ lb fat to 1 lb flour freezes satisfactorily. Biscuits which are cut out are difficult to store without damage and the easiest way to freeze the mixture is in rolls of the same diameter as the required biscuit. Several different flavours can be made from one large batch of mixture. Soft mixture can be piped before freezing.

Freeze—Wrap each roll individually in heavy duty foil and seal. Pipe or spoon soft biscuit mixtures on to a baking tray and freeze uncovered on the tray. When frozen lift off with a palette knife and pack in polythene bags or containers and seal.

Storage Life—Up to 6 months.

Thaw—Leave rolls of mixture in packaging at room temperature until sufficiently soft to cut into ⅛ inch thick slices. Bake as normal. Place frozen piped or spooned biscuits on a baking tray and bake at usual temperature, allowing about 5 minutes longer than normal.

Puddings

Sponge Puddings: Puddings made from plain or rich cake mixtures and quick mixes can be frozen equally well before or after steaming. Basins made of foil or polythene are the most suitable, but if only glass or earthenware basins are available line with greased foil and remove puddings from basins when frozen and seal in the usual way.

Freeze—Make puddings in the normal way adding flavourings and topping.

Uncooked Puddings: seal basins tightly with heavy duty foil and freeze immediately.

Cooked Puddings: cool thoroughly and seal basins with heavy duty foil.

Storage Life—Uncooked Puddings: up to 1 month. *Cooked Puddings:* up to 3 months.

Thaw—Remove packaging, cover top with greased foil and place frozen pudding in steamer.

Uncooked Puddings: 1½ pint pudding basin takes 2½ hours.

Cooked Puddings: 1½ pint pudding basin takes 45 minutes to thaw and heat through.

Fruit Charlotte

Freeze—Make up in a greased foil pie-dish or basin, seal tightly with heavy duty foil and freeze unbaked.

Storage Life—Up to 3 months.

Thaw—Leave overnight in a refrigerator then bake at Gas No. 5 or 375°F (191°C) for 45–60 minutes, or place frozen and uncovered in oven at above temperature, and bake for 1–1¼ hours until fruit is tender and top golden brown.

Summer Pudding: Can be frozen but it is usually more convenient to freeze the fruit separately and make when required, as the storage life of the fruit is much longer than the made-up pudding.

Freeze—Make in any basin, except metal or foil; cover top with plastic film, seal with foil.

Storage Life—Up to 1 month.

Thaw—Unpack, cover basin with a fitting plate, top with a heavy weight and leave overnight.

Bread and Butter Puddings: These are best frozen before cooking, but are difficult to handle as the dish must be kept level to avoid spilling custard until frozen. If frozen baked and then refreshed before serving the result is similar to a re-heated pudding.

Freeze—Make in a greased foil pie-dish, cover tightly with heavy duty foil and place carefully in freezer so that dish remains level until frozen.

Storage Life—Up to 1 month.

Thaw—Leave overnight in refrigerator and then bake as usual, or place frozen and uncovered in oven at Gas No. 3 or 325°F (163°C) for about 1¾ hours, until custard is set.

Batters

Yorkshire Pudding: No need to allow batter to stand; grease foil containers and two-thirds fill.

Freeze—Uncovered until firm, then package and seal.

Storage Life—3–4 months.

Thaw—Bake direct from frozen in hot oven allowing one third extra cooking time than if baking fresh batter.

Pancakes: Pancakes store very well. To prevent pancakes from becoming rubbery during freezing add one tablespoon of oil to the basic recipe.

Freeze—Pancakes must be cold before packing; to cool quickly and to allow the steam to escape slip cooked pancakes on to a wire cooling tray; if you will want to remove only a few pancakes at a time interleave them with greaseproof paper or polythene sheets. Seal tightly in stacks in polythene bags or wrapped in heavy duty foil.

Storage Life—Up to 2 months.

Thaw—Leave in packaging at room temperature for 2–3 hours, or overnight in the refrigerator;

for rapid thawing, unwrap, spread out singly and leave at room temperature for 15–20 minutes.

Re-heat—Place stack (4–5) of frozen pancakes wrapped in foil, in fairly hot oven, Gas No. 5 or 375°F (191°C) for 20–30 minutes, or heat individual pancakes in a lightly greased heated frying pan, about half a minute each side.

Filled Pancakes: Pancakes filled with sweet or savoury fillings freeze well provided the fillings also freeze well, *e.g.* avoid fillings containing hard-boiled eggs and sliced tomato as a garnish.

Remember also not to overseason savoury fillings.

Freeze—Place in greased foil dish and seal with heavy duty foil.

Storage Life—Up to 1–2 months.

Thaw—Place frozen, in packaging, in fairly hot oven Gas No. 6 or 400°F (204°C) for 30 minutes.

Note

Alternatively, the fillings and pancakes can be frozen separately and assembled after thawing.

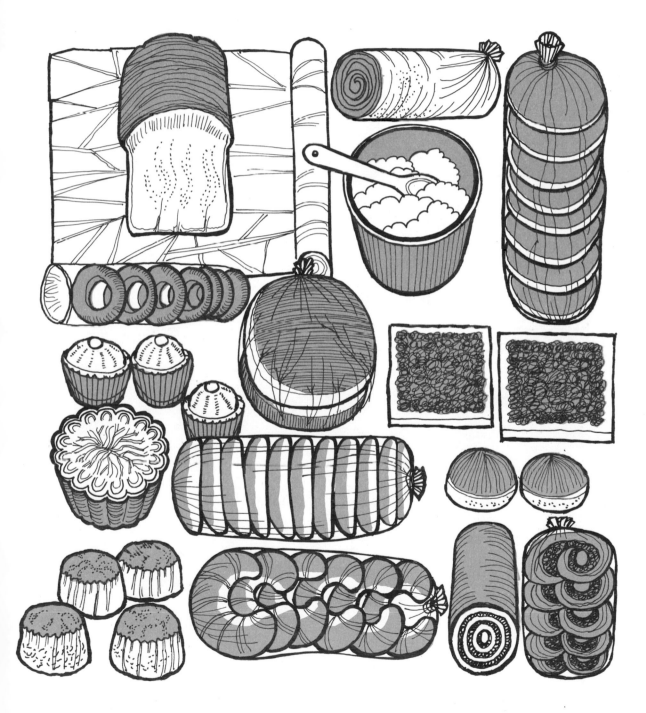

PART 2

Recipes

My aim in this recipe section is to inspire you to cook interesting imaginative dishes using the products in your freezer, making this a *from* the freezer cook book rather than a *for* the freezer cook book.

Market research tells us that although the freezer satisfies many differing household needs, the chief reason for purchase is to buy commercially frozen foods in bulk at reduced prices. Here is a selection of recipes showing uses for frozen foods other than their prime function. With a freezer well stocked with a variety of foodstuffs, a meal can always be instantly provided without worry or effort. Of course, it is always worthwhile freezing a portion of any of your favourite recipes so that one effort of making provides for two (or more) enjoyable meals.

Meat & Meat Products

TASTY STEAK

Serves 4

Cooking Time: 30 minutes
Temperature: Gas No. 6 or 400°F (204°C)

FROM THE FREEZER

4 rump or sirloin steaks

1. Thaw steaks about 2 hours at room temperature.

FROM THE STORECUPBOARD

1 oz butter
2 oz onion, chopped
2 oz celery, chopped
2 level tablespoons brown sugar
1 level tablespoon mustard
2 level teaspoons salt
1 level teaspoon paprika
1 level tablespoon tomato purée
2 tablespoons Worcestershire sauce
2 tablespoons vinegar
2 tablespoons lemon juice
¼ pint water

2. Brown steaks in butter in frying pan. Remove to 2½ pint oven-proof dish.
3. Gently fry onion and celery in remaining butter until onion is pale golden.
4. Add all dry ingredients to pan and then all liquid ones.
5. Pour sauce mixture over steaks and cover with lid or foil.
6. Bake in fairly hot oven until steak is quite tender.
7. Serve steak in its sauce with boiled rice.

Note

1. Tougher cuts of steak may be used with correspondingly longer cooking time.
2. May be cooked, cooled and frozen.
3. Storage time in freezer: 3–4 weeks.

HIGHLAND STEAK

Serves 4

Cooking Time: approximately 1 hour

FROM THE FREEZER

4 rump steaks
4–5 oz cream

1. Thaw steaks just long enough to be able to remove fat and cut into thin strips.
2. Thaw completely overnight in refrigerator in marinade, made by mixing together oil, salt, pepper and Worcestershire sauce (see below).
3. Thaw cream about 2 hours at room temperature or overnight in refrigerator.

FROM THE STORECUPBOARD

3 tablespoons oil
½ level teaspoon salt
Freshly milled pepper
1 teaspoon Worcestershire sauce
¼ pint milk
2 tablespoons whisky
1 level tablespoon flour
8 oz mushrooms, sliced

4. Mix cream and milk together.
5. Gently fry steaks and marinade in deep frying pan for 5–6 minutes.
6. Pour over whisky and flame.
7. Add half cream/milk, and cover with lid or foil and simmer for about 20 minutes.
8. Blend flour with rest of cream/milk.
9. Add to frying pan with mushrooms. Adjust seasonings.
10. Simmer for 20–25 minutes until tender.
11. Serve with plain boiled rice, garnished with chopped parsley.

Note

1. May also be served with tossed green salad.

BOEUF STROGONOFF

Serves 4

Cooking Time: Approximately 10–15 minutes

FROM THE FREEZER

4 rump steaks
½ pint cream

1. Thaw steaks and cream about 2 hours at room temperature.

FROM THE STORECUPBOARD

4 oz butter
1 onion, finely chopped
8 oz button mushrooms, thinly sliced
Salt and pepper
1 tablespoon lemon juice

2. Cut each rump steak into ½ inch strips.
3. Melt half butter in heavy based frying pan and fry onion until transparent.
4. Add strips of steak and fry for about 5 minutes until tender.
5. Remove steak, add rest of butter and cook mushrooms.
6. Replace steak and season to taste.
7. Stir lemon juice into cream and pour into pan and heat through carefully.
8. Serve with border of boiled rice, garnished with a little chopped parsley.

HOMESPUN LOAF

Serves 2 to 4

Cooking Time: 1 hour
Temperature: Gas No. 4 or 350°F (177°C)

FROM THE FREEZER

1 lb minced beef
8 oz sausage meat

1. Thaw minced beef and sausage meat overnight in refrigerator.

FROM THE STORECUPBOARD

8 oz potatoes
1 large onion
1 cooking apple
1 egg
3 tablespoons milk
2 level teaspoons salt
¼ level teaspoon pepper

2. Peel and grate potatoes, onion and apple.
3. Mix in all other ingredients until evenly blended.
4. Pack into 2 greased 1 lb loaf tins.
5. Bake in moderate oven.
6. Leave 5 minutes to set before turning out.
7. Serve 1 loaf hot. Cool other quickly, wrap in foil and freeze.

Note

1. Storage time in freezer: 2 months.

PORK CHOP WITH APRICOTS

Serves 4

Cooking Time: 30–40 minutes

FROM THE FREEZER

4 pork chops
8 apricot halves
3 tablespoons green peas

1. Thaw chops in refrigerator for about 3 hours.
2. Use apricots and peas from frozen.

FROM THE STORECUPBOARD

1 oz seasoned flour
1 oz lard or pork dripping
1 small onion, chopped
1 tablespoon Soy sauce
¼ pint fruit juice, stock or wine

3. Toss pork chops in seasoned flour.
4. Melt lard in frying pan and brown chops.
5. Add onion, Soy sauce and fruit juice.
6. Simmer 15–20 minutes depending on thickness of chop.
7. Add peas and cook for further 5–10 minutes.
8. Garnish each chop with 2 apricot halves. Pour sauce over and serve.

Note

1. May be cooked, cooled and frozen, but as quick to cook as above.
2. Storage time in freezer: 6–8 weeks.

PORK CHOPS IN CIDER

Serves 4

Cooking Time: 30–35 minutes
Temperature: Gas No. 4 or 350°F
(177°C)

FROM THE FREEZER

4 pork chops

1. Thaw pork chops at least 3 hours or overnight in refrigerator.

FROM THE STORECUPBOARD

2 level tablespoons any favourite packet stuffing
4 small cooking apples
1 level tablespoon cornflour
½ pint cider
Salt and pepper

2. Make up packet stuffing as directed on packet.
3. Core apples and fill cavity with stuffing.
4. Brown chops in frying pan and place in shallow ovenproof dish.
5. Stir cornflour into pan juices and gradually add cider. Stir until thickened and smooth.
6. Add salt and pepper to taste and pour sauce over pork chops.
7. Cover with lid or foil and bake in moderate oven with apples.
8. Serve cidered pork chops garnished with apples.

SWEET AND SOUR PORK

Serves 4

Cooking Time: Approximately 30 minutes

FROM THE FREEZER

8 thick rashers of belly pork
Sweet and Sour Sauce (see page 91)

1. Thaw rashers of pork about 3 hours in refrigerator.
2. Thaw sauce by gently reheating from frozen.

FROM THE STORECUPBOARD

½ lb self-raising flour
1–2 eggs

1 tablespoon oil
½ pint beer
½ lb noodles

3. Grill belly pork rashers for 10 minutes each side under moderate heat.
4. Allow to cool, discard excess fat and cut in bite-size pieces.
5. Make up fritter batter in usual way using first four storecupboard ingredients.
6. Dip pork pieces in batter and deep fat fry until puffed and golden brown.
7. Drain on absorbent kitchen paper.
8. Cook noodles in boiling salted water for about 7 minutes.
9. Place pork fritters on bed of noodles.
10. Pour over a little of sauce. Serve rest separately.

Note

1. Whole dish may be prepared for freezer.
2. Cook pork in deep fat until batter has just set.
3. Drain, cool and freeze.
4. Allow to almost thaw before frying as above.
5. Storage time in freezer: 4–5 weeks.

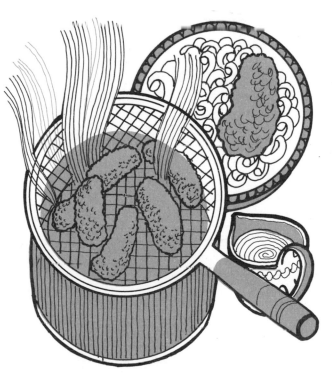

CREAMED LAMB CHOPS

Serves 4

Cooking Time: 45–50 minutes
Temperature: Gas No. 4 or 350°F (177°C)

FROM THE FREEZER

8 small lamb chops
4–5 oz cream

1. Thaw lamb chops and cream about 2 hours at room temperature.

FROM THE STORECUPBOARD

1 tablespoon oil
1 tablespoon vinegar
1 tablespoon Worcestershire sauce
$\frac{1}{2}$ level teaspoon salt
$\frac{1}{4}$ level teaspoon pepper
Dash paprika
2 bay leaves

2. Brown lamb chops in oil in frying pan.
3. Arrange chops in shallow $2\frac{1}{2}$–3 pint ovenproof dish.
4. Stir all remaining ingredients, except bay leaves, into pan juices.
5. Pour over chops, top with bay leaves and cover with lid or foil.
6. Bake in moderate oven.
7. Serve chops with juices spooned over.

LAMB CHOPS WITH PINEAPPLE-MINT SAUCE

Serves 4

Cooking Time: 10–20 minutes

FROM THE FREEZER

4 lamb chops
4 chopped mint cubes

1. Thaw lamb chops 2–3 hours at room temperature.
2. Use mint from frozen.

FROM THE STORECUPBOARD

$\frac{1}{2}$ ($7\frac{1}{2}$ oz) can crushed pineapple
1 knob butter

3. Grill or fry chops until cooked.
4. Put crushed pineapple and butter in pan.
5. Add 4 mint cubes (see page 26) or 2 tablespoons of freshly chopped mint.
6. Gently heat through and serve over chops.
7. Serve with new potatoes and peas or beans.

Note

1. If chops are cooked from frozen, allow extra 10–15 minutes cooking time.

BRAISED LAMB CUTLETS

Serves 4

Cooking Time: $\frac{3}{4}$–1 hour
Temperature: Gas No. 4 or 350°F (177°C)

FROM THE FREEZER

4 lamb cutlets
$\frac{1}{2}$ pint stock

1. Thaw lamb cutlets and stock 2–3 hours at room temperature.

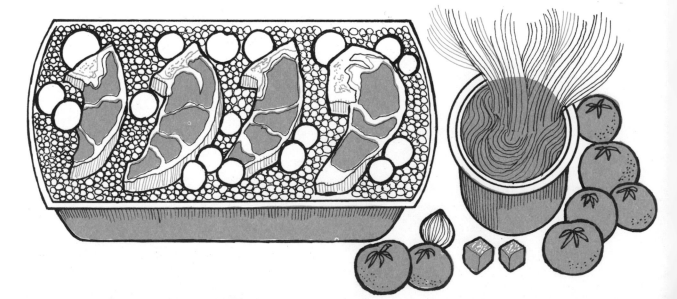

FROM THE STORECUPBOARD

1 oz dripping
1 small onion, thinly sliced
1 large potato, thinly sliced
Salt and pepper
8 tomatoes, skinned and sliced
Pinch mixed herbs
8 rashers streaky bacon, de-rinded
Parsley

2. Fry cutlets in dripping, browning each side.
3. Grease $2\frac{1}{2}$ pint ovenproof dish. Cover base with half the sliced onion and potato, and season.
4. Place cutlets on onion and potato, and cover with remainder of mixture.
5. Place sliced tomatoes on top, and add stock and herbs.
6. Cover top with bacon rashers.
7. Bake uncovered in moderate oven.
8. Sprinkle with a little chopped parsley.

Note

1. May be cooked, cooled and frozen.
2. When preparing for freezer, cook in lidded dish without bacon.
3. To reheat, allow to thaw overnight in refrigerator, place bacon rashers on top and heat in moderate oven for 25–35 minutes.
4. Storage time in freezer: 4–6 weeks.

WEST INDIAN LAMB

Serves 4 to 6

Cooking Time: 30–40 minutes.

FROM THE FREEZER

3 lb leg or shoulder lamb

1. Thaw lamb overnight in refrigerator or 5–6 hours at room temperature.

FROM THE STORECUPBOARD

2 oz butter
2 tablespoons olive oil
1 level tablespoon curry powder
$\frac{1}{2}$ level teaspoon ground ginger
$\frac{1}{2}$ level teaspoon cayenne
$\frac{1}{2}$ level teaspoon turmeric
Salt and pepper
2 tablespoons lemon juice
$\frac{1}{2}$ pint stock

2. Remove lamb from bone. Put bones to simmer for stock.
3. Cut meat in bite-size cubes.
4. Fry lamb in butter and oil until golden brown.
5. Add curry powder, ground ginger, cayenne, turmeric, salt, pepper and lemon juice, and stir well.
6. Add stock to just cover meat.
7. Cover with lid or foil. Simmer for about 30 minutes or until lamb is tender.
8. Serve with boiled rice, fried bananas and chutney.

Note

1. May be cooked, cooled and frozen.
2. Allow to thaw before reheating.
3. Storage time in freezer: 4–5 weeks.

PORK SAUSAGES IN ORANGE SAUCE

Serves 4

Cooking Time: 20 minutes

FROM THE FREEZER

1 lb pork sausages
$\frac{1}{2}$ can orange juice

1. Thaw sausages about 2 hours at room temperature.
2. Use orange juice from frozen.

FROM THE STORECUPBOARD

2 onions, thinly sliced
2 tablespoons vinegar
2 tablespoons red currant jelly
1 orange, peeled and sliced

3. Brown sausages in frying pan and pour away any excess fat.
4. Add onions, vinegar, red currant jelly and orange juice made up to $\frac{1}{2}$ pint with water.
5. Simmer for 20 minutes.
6. Serve garnished with fresh orange segments and creamed potatoes.

Note

1. The orange sauce is also delicious with roast pork.
2. Sausages may be cooked from frozen with increased cooking time.
3. Cooked dish may be frozen, but as quick to prepare as above.

DANISH CABBAGE CAKE

Serves 4

Cooking Time: 45 minutes
Temperature: Gas No. 6 or 400°F
(204°C)

FROM THE FREEZER

1 lb pork sausages
4–5 oz cream

1. Thaw sausages and cream about 2 hours at room temperature.

FROM THE STORECUPBOARD

1 firm white cabbage
Pinch sage
Salt and pepper
1 egg yolk
Chopped parsley

2. Separate cabbage leaves and parboil for 4–5 minutes.
3. Grease bottom and sides of deep 2½ pint ovenproof dish.
4. Remove skins from sausages. Mix sausage meat with herbs and seasonings in basin.
5. Line dish with cabbage leaves.
6. Fill dish with alternate layers of cabbage leaves and sausage meat, ending with layer of cabbage leaves.
7. Cover with lid or foil. Place dish in tray of water and bake in fairly hot oven.
8. To make sauce, drain off any liquid, add egg yolk and cream, and reheat gently.
9. Turn out cabbage cake on to serving plate, pour sauce over and sprinkle with a little chopped parsley.
10. Serve cut into wedges.

BEEF SAUSAGE RISOTTO

Serves 4

Cooking Time: Simmer 30–40 minutes

FROM THE FREEZER

12 skinless beef sausages
3 oz mixed vegetables

1. Use sausages and vegetables from frozen.

FROM THE STORECUPBOARD

2 tablespoons cooking oil
1 large onion, chopped
9 oz long grain rice
1 pint stock, made from beef stock cube, pineapple juice and water
6 oz button mushrooms
1 green pepper, chopped
3 pineapple rings, chopped
Salt and pepper

2. Cut each sausage in 4.
3. Fry in oil for about 5 minutes until brown. Remove sausages from pan.
4. Add remaining oil, and fry onion and rice for a few minutes.
5. Add stock and bring to boil.
6. Return sausages and all other ingredients.
7. Cover with lid or foil and simmer for 30–40 minutes until all liquid is absorbed and rice is cooked.

Note

1. Sausages may be replaced by diced beefburger, cooked chicken, prawns; pineapple by peaches, apricots, apples; vegetables by celery, tomatoes, etc.
2. Whole dish may be cooked, cooled and frozen.
3. Storage time in freezer: 1–2 months.

BEER SAUSAGE BAKE

Serves 4

Cooking Time: 15 minutes
Temperature: Gas No. 6 or 400°F
(204°C)

FROM THE FREEZER

1 lb pork sausages

1. Thaw sausages about 2 hours at room temperature.

FROM THE STORECUPBOARD

2 apples, peeled and cored
2 onions, sliced
1 level dessertspoon flour
½ pint light ale
1 chicken stock cube
Salt and pepper
1 packet instant potato (4–5 servings)

structed. Spread on top of apples and onions to cover completely.

9. Bake in fairly hot oven until potato browns.

Note

1. May be prepared, cooled and frozen.
2. Storage time in freezer: 1–2 months.

BEEFBURGER PIE

Serves 2

Cooking Time: 20–25 minutes
Temperature: Gas No. 7 or 425 °F (218 °C)

FROM THE FREEZER

4 beefburgers
$7\frac{1}{2}$ oz puff pastry
2 oz grated Cheddar cheese

1. Thaw beefburgers and pastry about 1 hour at room temperature.
2. Use cheese from frozen.

FROM THE STORECUPBOARD

$\frac{1}{4}$ white cabbage, finely chopped
1 clove garlic, crushed and finely chopped (optional)
Salt and pepper
Beaten egg or milk for glazing

3. Line 7 inch flan ring with two-thirds of pastry, leaving $\frac{1}{2}$ inch overhang.
4. Place beefburgers in flan case and cover with mixture of cabbage, garlic, cheese and seasonings.
5. Roll out remaining pastry to 7 inch circle for lid, dampen edges of overhang, place lid on top and seal well. Flute edges.
6. Make 6 radial slits from centre of lid. Brush round centre with egg or milk and fold back from the centre to make star shape.
7. Brush pie with egg or milk.
8. Bake in hot oven, removing flan ring after 15 minutes.

Note

1. May be made in foil shallow pie dish, but would have to be served in the dish, because of decorative open top.
2. Flan ring allows pastry to be browned on outside.

2. Brown sausages for 5–10 minutes in frying pan. Remove to oven-proof dish.
3. Cook apples and onions in sausage fat until softened.
4. Spoon over sausages.
5. Add flour to about 1 tablespoon of remaining fat in pan.
6. Add ale and stock cube, and bring to boil to thicken. Season.
7. Pour over sausage mix.
8. Make up mashed potato as in-

BEEFBURGER MEDALS

Serves 4

Cooking Time: 10–15 minutes

FROM THE FREEZER

1 packet pâté de foie
4 beefburgers
4 croûtons of fried bread about
  3½ inches in diameter (see page
  32)

1. Thaw pâté ½ hour at room temperature.
2. Use beefburgers and croûtons from frozen.

FROM THE STORECUPBOARD

2 rashers streaky bacon
1 tomato, skinned
Parsley

3. With streaky bacon make bacon rolls by stretching each rasher, using back of knife, until twice its length and half its thickness.
4. Cut in half, and roll round a finger.
5. Skewer bacon rolls to stop them

unwinding and bake in oven, grill or fry.
6. Grill, fry or bake beefburgers.
7. Place beefburger topped with slice of tomato on fried bread.
8. Pipe pâté de foie on to tomato, and top with bacon roll and tiny sprig of parsley.

Note

1. Beefburgers, fried bread and bacon rolls can be stored in freezer and placed, unassembled, straight in oven whilst you prepare pâté, etc.
2. Storage time in freezer: bacon rolls, 6 weeks; croûtons, 4 weeks.

PANCAKE TOWER

Serves 4

Cooking Time: 25–30 minutes
Temperature: Gas No. 8 or 450°F
(232°C)

FROM THE FREEZER

5 thin pancakes
9½ oz packet cooked savoury
  mince with vegetables and
  gravy
½ pint cheese sauce
1 oz grated Cheddar cheese

1. Packet of 5 pancakes will separate in about ½ hour in warm kitchen.
2. Cooked minced beef can be thawed more quickly in oven.
3. Thaw sauce by heating gently.
4. Use cheese from frozen.
5. Place 1 pancake on ovenproof serving plate.
6. Cover with one quarter of mince, another pancake and so on ending with a pancake.
7. Coat with sauce and sprinkle with grated cheese.
8. Bake in very hot oven until bubbly and brown.
9. Serve cut into wedges.

Note

1. If fresh ingredients are used, whole dish may be made, assembled and frozen.
2. Reheating takes about 1 hour from frozen or as above if allowed to thaw.
3. Storage time in freezer: 6–8 weeks.

WEST COUNTRY BOLOGNESE

Serves 4

Cooking Time: Simmer for 20 minutes

FROM THE FREEZER

2 (9½ oz) packets cooked savoury mince with vegetables and gravy
2 oz grated Cheddar cheese

1. Use savoury minced beef and cheese from frozen.

FROM THE STORECUPBOARD

1 glass white wine
8 oz can tomatoes
1 level teaspoon sugar
Salt and pepper
A little grated nutmeg
1 clove garlic, crushed and chopped
8 oz spaghetti

2. Take mince from containers, place in pan with wine and tomatoes, and thaw slowly over low heat.
3. When completely thawed, add all seasonings, bring to boil and simmer gently for about 20 minutes.
4. Cook spaghetti 10–15 minutes in fast boiling salted water. Drain.
5. Pour sauce over cooked spaghetti, top with cheese and serve.

Note

1. If raw mince is used whole dish may be cooked, cooled and frozen.
2. Thaw before reheating.
3. Storage time in freezer: 6–8 weeks.

BAKED MEAT ROLL

Serves 4

Cooking Time: 35–45 minutes
Temperature: Gas No. 6 or 400°F (204°C)

FROM THE FREEZER

9½ oz packet cooked savoury minced beef in gravy
13½ oz packet puff pastry
4 beefburgers

1. Thaw minced beef about 2 hours at room temperature.

2. Thaw pastry and beefburgers about 1 hour at room temperature.
3. Better to thaw all 3 overnight in refrigerator.

FROM THE STORECUPBOARD
Beaten egg for glazing

4. Roll out pastry thinly in a rectangle.
5. Spread minced beef over pastry.
6. Cut beefburgers into strips and place on minced beef.
7. Roll up as for Swiss roll.
8. Brush with egg glaze.
9. Make pastry leaves from trimmings for garnish.
10. Bake in fairly hot oven.

BAKED PÂTÉ ROLLS

Serves 4

Cooking Time: 15 minutes
Temperature: Gas No. 7 or 425°F (218°C)

FROM THE FREEZER
2 (4 oz) packets pâté de foie
8 slices from large thinly sliced loaf

1. Thaw pâté and bread about 30 minutes at room temperature.

FROM THE STORECUPBOARD
Melted butter or margarine

2. Remove crusts from bread and roll slices with rolling pin.
3. Divide pâté into 8 and spread each portion evenly on bread.
4. Roll up like Swiss roll.
5. Brush over with melted butter.
6. Bake in hot oven until crisp and golden brown.

Note

1. If seam of roll is placed underneath, rolls should not unwind or need cocktail stick to secure.
2. May be prepared with fresh pâté and bread, and frozen before baking.
3. Cook straight from frozen allowing a few extra minutes.
4. For cocktail parties, cut each roll into 3 with sharp knife. Serve hot piled on platter garnished with watercress.

Chicken

JEWISH LIVER PÂTÉ

Serves 6 for starters

Cooking Time: 5–10 minutes

FROM THE FREEZER

¾ lb chicken liver

1. Thaw chicken liver 2–3 hours at room temperature.

FROM THE STORECUPBOARD

3 oz margarine
½ Spanish onion
2 hard-boiled eggs
1 stalk celery, finely chopped
¼ green pepper, finely chopped
Salt and pepper

2. Cook liver in margarine for a few minutes until firm.
3. Remove liver from pan. Cook onion until transparent.
4. Put hard-boiled eggs, liver and onion through fine mincer.
5. Combine with celery, green pepper, salt and pepper.
6. Serve with toast.

Note

1. Unsuitable for freezing as hard-boiled eggs will become leathery.

CHICKEN LIVER PÂTÉ

Serves 6 to 8

Cooking Time: 8 minutes

FROM THE FREEZER

½ lb chicken liver

1. Thaw chicken liver 1–2 hours at room temperature.

FROM THE STORECUPBOARD

3 oz unsalted butter
1 onion, chopped
1 clove garlic (optional)
4 oz streaky bacon, chopped

1 tablespoon chopped parsley
¼ teaspoon chopped thyme
1 tablespoon brandy
1 teaspoon lemon juice
Salt and pepper
Extra melted butter

2. Trim any fibrous parts from liver.
3. Fry onion and garlic in 1 oz butter for 5 minutes.
4. Add liver, bacon and herbs, and cook for 3 minutes.
5. Add remaining butter to melt.
6. Sieve liver mixture, or liquidize or pound with pestle and mortar.
7. Add brandy, lemon juice and seasoning.
8. Pack into oiled mould or individual pots. Top with melted butter.
9. Chill well before serving.

Note

1. Freezes well.
2. Set shape in mould in freezer, unmould and wrap in foil.
3. If whole will not be required at one time, section off slices with pieces of foil.
4. Storage time in freezer: 4 weeks.

AMERICAN BAKED CHICKEN OR TURKEY SALAD

Serves 4

Cooking time: 25–35 minutes
Temperature: Gas No. 8 or 450°F (232°C)

FROM THE FREEZER

14 oz cooked chicken or turkey

1. If meat is on carcass allow to thaw overnight in refrigerator.
2. If already cut up allow 2–3 hours at room temperature.

FROM THE STORECUPBOARD

2 (10½ oz) cans condensed chicken soup

2 cups celery, chopped
1 small onion, finely chopped
1 cup walnuts, chopped
1 level teaspoon salt
1 level teaspoon pepper
2 tablespoons lemon juice
1½ cups mayonnaise
4 hard-boiled eggs, roughly
  chopped
4 cups potato crisps, crushed
Chopped parsley for garnish

3. If meat is on carcass, remove, and cut in bite-size pieces.
4. Combine all ingredients together, except potato crisps and parsley.
5. Place in shallow 2½ pint ovenproof dish. Cover with lid or foil.
6. Bake in pre-heated very hot oven for 20—30 minutes.
7. Remove lid or foil. Cover with crushed potato crisps and return to oven for about 5 minutes until crisps begin to brown.
8. Garnish with a little chopped parsley.

Note

1. Cup measurements are used because proportions of one ingredient to another are more important than exact quantities.
2. Unsuitable for freezing because of hard-boiled eggs and mayonnaise.
3. Good and interesting way of using up remains of the chicken or turkey.

COQ EN BRIOCHE

Serves 6

Cooking Time: 30 minutes
Temperature: Gas No. 6 or 400 °F
(204 °C)

FROM THE FREEZER

½ (3 lb) chicken breast roll
13 oz packet puff pastry
4 oz pâté de foie

1. Halve 3 lb chicken roll with freezer knife, rewrap half not being used and return to freezer.
2. Thaw half to be used overnight in refrigerator.
3. Thaw pastry and pâté overnight in refrigerator or 1—2 hours at room temperature.

FROM THE STORECUPBOARD

4 oz mushrooms, thinly sliced
1 beaten egg for glazing

4. Roll out pastry to rectangle approximately 15 by 12 inches.
5. Spread pâté over pastry to within 1 inch from edge all round.
6. Scatter mushrooms over pâté.
7. Cut chicken roll in half lengthways. Place the 2 pieces end to end to make 12 inch chicken roll with flat base on prepared pastry.
8. Parcel up, sealing ends well. Have long join of pastry underneath.
9. Decorate top with pastry leaves made from pastry trimmings.
10. Brush whole with beaten egg.
11. Bake in fairly hot oven until pastry is cooked and golden brown.
12. Serve hot or cold.

Note

1. All ingredients inside pastry are cooked. You are only cooking the pastry.

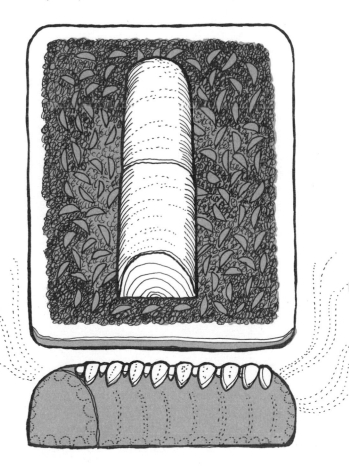

HAWAIIAN CHICKEN

Serves 4

Cooking Time: 10–15 minutes

FROM THE FREEZER

8 oz cooked chicken

1. Thaw chicken 1–2 hours at room temperature.

FROM THE STORECUPBOARD

1 fresh pineapple
1 oz butter
1 onion, chopped
1 green pepper, de-seeded and chopped
$\frac{1}{4}$ pint stock or water
2 teaspoons brown sugar
1 tablespoon vinegar
2 teaspoons Soy sauce
2 level teaspoons cornflour
Salt and pepper

2. Slice pineapple in half lengthways.
3. Scoop out pineapple flesh, reserving as much juice as possible, and chop finely.
4. Fry onion and pepper gently in butter.
5. Add pineapple juice made up to $\frac{1}{2}$ pint with stock or water.
6. Cut cooked chicken into bite-size pieces.
7. Add to pan with sugar, vinegar and Soy sauce.

8. Blend cornflour to paste with a little water.
9. Stir into pan to thicken sauce.
10. Season to taste.
11. Divide mixture between 2 half pineapple shells and serve on bed of boiled rice.

Note

1. Canned pineapple may be used. Pile mixture into frozen pineapple shells straight from freezer.

NEAPOLITAN CHICKEN

Serves 4

Cooking Time: 30–35 minutes
Temperature: Gas No. 7 or 425°F (218°C)

FROM THE FREEZER

1 lb cooked chicken
4–5 oz cream
4 oz grated Cheddar cheese

1. Thaw chicken and cream about 2 hours at room temperature.
2. Use cheese from frozen.

FROM THE STORECUPBOARD

$\frac{1}{2}$ lb spaghetti rings
4 oz butter
6 oz mushrooms, sliced
1 tablespoon lemon juice
2 oz almonds, flaked
1 tablespoon flour

½ level teaspoon salt
¼ level teaspoon pepper
⅛ teaspoon paprika
Pinch nutmeg
1 glass sherry
¾ pint chicken stock

3. Cook spaghetti rings as directed. Drain and place in 3 pint ovenproof dish.
4. Fry mushrooms in 2 oz butter until soft. Add lemon juice and place on top of spaghetti.
5. Sprinkle almonds on top of mushrooms.
6. Melt remaining 2 oz butter. Add flour and seasonings to make roux.
7. Gradually stir in sherry and chicken stock.
8. Bring to boil, stirring to thicken, and add cream.
9. Add diced cooked chicken and pour over spaghetti mixture.
10. Cover with layer of grated cheese.
11. Bake in hot oven until bubbly brown.

Note

1. May be prepared using fresh ingredients, chilled and frozen.
2. Storage time in freezer: 6–8 weeks.

CHICKEN SALAMAGUNDY

Serves 6–8

Cooking Time: None

FROM THE FREEZER

2 lb cooked chicken meat
4–5 oz cream

1. Thaw chicken and cream about 2 hours at room temperature.

FROM THE STORECUPBOARD

¼ pint mayonnaise
1 tablespoon chopped parsley
1 bunch spring onions
1 lemon
Salt and pepper
2 hard-boiled eggs
1 lettuce
¼ pint French dressing
1 bunch radishes
½ cucumber, sliced
1 bunch watercress

2. Whip cream until just thick.
3. Stir into mayonnaise with parsley and 1 tablespoon chopped spring onions.
4. Slice breast meat into strips. Dice any brown meat.
5. Peel lemon and chop inside flesh. Mix with diced and sliced chicken, and add to mayonnaise and cream mixture. Season well.
6. Pile in centre of large platter.
7. Chop egg whites and sieve egg yolks, and use to decorate chicken mixture.
8. Surround chicken mixture with shredded lettuce, tossed in French dressing.
9. Place radishes, cucumber and watercress around dish for decoration.

COCK-A-LEEKIE SOUP

Serves 4 to 6

Cooking Time: 2–2½ hours

FROM THE FREEZER

3 chicken joints

1. Use chicken from frozen.

FROM THE STORECUPBOARD

4 leeks
2 oz pearl barley
2½ pints water
1 level teaspoon salt
Freshly ground pepper
Bay leaf

2. Slice leeks in ½ inch rings.
3. Put all ingredients in heavy based pan.
4. Bring to boil. Simmer until chicken is cooked.
5. Remove from heat and cool.
6. Take out chicken portions, and discard skin and bones.
7. Chop chicken flesh into small pieces.
8. Remove any fat from cold soup.
9. Return chicken, bring to boil and serve.

Note

1. May be prepared, cooled and frozen.
2. Storage time in freezer: 2–4 months.

CRUNCHY CHICKEN

Serves 4

Cooking Time: 30–40 minutes
Temperature: Gas No. 6 or 400°F
(204°C)

FROM THE FREEZER

4 chicken portions
2 oz grated Cheddar cheese

1. Thaw chicken about 2 hours at room temperature.
2. Use cheese from frozen.

FROM THE STORECUPBOARD

Salt and pepper
2 oz butter
1 small onion, finely chopped
1 small packet potato crisps
2 tablespoons chopped parsley

3. Season chicken well.
4. Melt butter in pan. Add onion, crushed crisps and grated cheese.
5. Place chicken portions in roasting tin and coat each one evenly with crisps and onion mixture.
6. Place in fairly hot oven until chicken is cooked and topping golden brown and crisp.
7. Place $\frac{1}{2}$ tablespoon chopped parsley on each chicken portion and return to oven for 1–2 minutes.
8. Serve with sweet corn and croquette potatoes.

Note

1. Cooked chicken may be used with correspondingly less cooking time.
2. Sweet corn may be cooked straight from freezer in casserole in oven. Add seasoning and good knob of butter, cover and cook for 30–40 minutes.
3. Croquette potatoes should be placed at top of oven on baking sheets for 20–25 minutes.

CHICKEN PUDDING

Serves 4

Cooking Time: 2$\frac{1}{2}$–3 hours

FROM THE FREEZER

4 chicken portions

1. Thaw chicken 2–3 hours at room temperature.

FROM THE STORECUPBOARD

1 lb flour
1 level teaspoon salt
6 oz butter
4 egg yolks
Water
1 oz seasoned flour
4 oz boiled ham, chopped
4 oz button mushrooms, chopped
Salt and pepper
2 tablespoons chopped parsley
$\frac{1}{2}$ level teaspoon tarragon
$\frac{1}{2}$ level teaspoon rosemary
1 level teaspoon grated lemon rind
$\frac{1}{2}$ pint stock

2. Rub butter into flour and salt. Add egg yolks and sufficient water to mix to a firm dough.
3. Line well buttered 2$\frac{1}{2}$ pint basin with two-thirds of dough.
4. Cut chicken into small pieces, removing as many bones as possible.
5. Toss chicken pieces in seasoned flour.
6. Mix chicken, ham and mushrooms together with seasonings, herbs and lemon rind.
7. Place in lined basin, pour in stock and cover with lid, made from remaining pastry.
8. Dampen edges and pinch together.
9. Cover with buttered foil.
10. Steam for 2$\frac{1}{2}$–3 hours.

CITRUS CHICKEN

Serves 4

Cooking Time: 40–50 minutes
Temperature: Gas No. 4 or 350°F
(177°C)

FROM THE FREEZER

4 chicken portions for frying
4–5 oz cream

1. Thaw chicken and cream about 2 hours at room temperature.

FROM THE STORECUPBOARD

2 oz butter
1$\frac{1}{2}$ tablespoons dry sherry

1$\frac{1}{2}$ tablespoons dry white wine
Grated rind of orange
2 tablespoons lemon juice
Salt and pepper
Slices of fresh orange and lemon for garnish

2. Brown chicken portions in butter in frying pan for 5–10 minutes.
3. Place chicken portions in 3 pint ovenproof dish.
4. Add remaining storecupboard ingredients, except garnish, to pan juices. Bring to boil and pour over chicken.
5. Cover with lid or foil.
6. Bake for 30–40 minutes in a moderate oven.
7. Remove chicken to serving dish. Add cream to pan juices.
8. Heat through gently and pour over chicken.
9. Garnish each portion with orange and lemon twist.

Note

1. Grated orange rind could be in freezer.

CHICKEN IN A PARCEL

Serves 1

Cooking Time: 1 hour
Temperature: Gas No. 7 or 425°F
(218°C)

FROM THE FREEZER

1 chicken portion

1. Thaw chicken 2–3 hours at room temperature.

FROM THE STORECUPBOARD

1 oz butter
2–3 mushrooms
2–3 baby onions
2 tablespoons single cream or top of milk
1 tablespoon sherry
Salt and pepper

2. Brown chicken portion in butter in frying pan.
3. Place chicken with all above ingredients on piece of foil, parcel up loosely and bake in hot oven for 1 hour.

QUICK CHICKEN PROVENÇAL

Serves 4

Cooking Time: 1 hour
Temperature: Gas No. 5 or 375°F
(191°C)

FROM THE FREEZER

4 chicken portions

1. Thaw chicken 2–3 hours at room temperature.

FROM THE STORECUPBOARD

15 oz can spaghetti rings
15 oz can tomatoes
1 large onion, chopped
1 level teaspoon sugar
½ level teaspoon basil
Salt and pepper
1 wineglass sherry (optional)

2. Lay spaghetti rings in 2½ pint shallow ovenproof dish.
3. Mix together tomatoes, onion, sugar and basil, and place on top of spaghetti.
4. Place chicken portions on top. Sprinkle well with salt and pepper.
5. Cover with lid or foil and bake in fairly hot oven for 45 minutes.
6. Remove lid or foil. Add sherry and bake for 15 minutes to crisp skin.

Note

1. May be cooked, cooled and frozen.
2. Storage time in freezer: 2–3 months.

CHICKEN BREASTS WITH PÂTÉ

Serves 4

Cooking Time: Approximately
10 minutes

FROM THE FREEZER

4 cooked chicken breast portions
4–5 oz cream
2 oz pâté de foie

1. Thaw chicken, cream and pâté about 2 hours at room temperature.

FROM THE STORECUPBOARD

1 oz butter
2 tablespoons brandy (optional)

2. Heat through chicken in butter.
3. Add brandy, and flame. Remove from pan and keep warm.
4. Stir pâté and blend with cream.
5. Pour cream mixture into pan and gently combine with meat juice to heat through.
6. Serve chicken on bed of cooked spaghetti and pour sauce over.

ROAST DUCKLING

Serves 4

Cooking Time: 45–60 minutes
Temperature: Gas No. 4 or 350°F
(177°C)

FROM THE FREEZER

4 cooked duck portions
4 large slices fried bread

1. Use duck and fried bread from frozen.

FROM THE STORECUPBOARD

¼ pint red wine
8 oz can cherries
Salt and pepper
1 clove garlic
½ oz cornflour
Watercress

2. Place duck portions in casserole.
3. Pour in red wine, juice and stoned cherries.
4. Season with salt, pepper and garlic.
5. Cover with lid and heat through in moderate oven.
6. Warm frozen fried bread in oven.
7. Blend cornflour with a little water.
8. Remove duckling to serving plate and keep warm.
9. Pour pan liquor on to cornflour to blend, and return to pan to cook and thicken.
10. Put each duck portion on to piece of fried bread. Pour over sauce with cherries.
11. Garnish with watercress.

SHRIMP STUFFED CHICKEN

Serves 6 to 8

Cooking Time: 1½ hours
Temperature: Gas No. 4 or 350°F
(177°C)

FROM THE FREEZER

4½ lb roasting chicken
4—5 oz cream
2 (2 oz) cartons potted shrimps
4 tablespoons peas
4 tablespoons chopped parsley
8 slices bread

1. Thaw chicken and cream overnight in refrigerator.
2. Use shrimps, peas, parsley and bread from frozen.

FROM THE STORECUPBOARD

Salt and pepper
½ level teaspoon marjoram
2 eggs, separated
2 oz butter, melted

3. Remove giblets from chicken, wash and wipe dry with absorbent kitchen paper. Rub a little salt and marjoram on inside of bird.

4. Lightly toast bread and soak for 5 minutes in cream.
5. Remove butter from potted shrimps and melt. Add bread and cream mixture, and stir constantly over low heat until smooth.
6. Allow to cool for 10 minutes.
7. Beat in egg yolks one at a time. Add shrimps, peas and parsley.
8. Whisk egg whites until stiff.
9. Carefully combine shrimp mixture with egg whites.
10. Season well, and fill breast and body cavity of chicken loosely with stuffing.
11. Secure skin and place in roasting pan. Brush all over with melted butter.
12. Roast in moderate oven, basting frequently.

Note

1. Use chicken liver for recipes page 46 or make giblet stock or gravy.

Fish & Shellfish

WHITE FISH COCKTAIL

Serves 4

Cooking Time: None

FROM THE FREEZER

1 lb cod

1. Thaw cod about 1 hour at room temperature.

FROM THE STORECUPBOARD

2 lemons
4 tomatoes, skinned
1 green pepper
4 tablespoons olive oil
1—2 tablespoons wine vinegar
4 tablespoons parsley, finely chopped
½ level teaspoon marjoram
Shake Tabasco sauce
Salt and pepper
Anchovy fillets

2. Skin and dice cod.
3. Marinate cod in juice of 2 lemons for at least 3 hours.
4. De-seed and dice tomatoes and pepper.
5. Add tomatoes, pepper, oil and vinegar to fish.
6. Stir in parsley, marjoram and Tabasco sauce. Add salt and pepper to taste.
7. Serve chilled, garnished with anchovy fillets.

COD PORTUGUESE

Serves 4

Cooking Time: 20–25 minutes
Temperature: Gas No. 4 or 350°F
(177°C)

FROM THE FREEZER

4 cod steaks
2 oz grated Cheddar cheese

1. Use cod and cheese from frozen.

FROM THE STORECUPBOARD

1 tablespoon lemon juice
Salt and pepper
2 tomatoes, skinned and sliced
2 oz mushrooms, sliced

2. Place cod in buttered $2\frac{1}{2}$ pint shallow ovenproof dish, and sprinkle with lemon juice and seasonings.
3. Add sliced tomatoes and mushrooms.
4. Cover with grated cheese.
5. Bake in moderate oven.

Note
1. Cooked dish may be frozen, but as quick to prepare as above.

COD AND SWEET CORN PIE

Serves 4

Cooking Time: 30 minutes
Temperature: Gas No. 5 or 375°F
(191°C)

FROM THE FREEZER

$13\frac{1}{2}$ oz packet pastry (either shortcrust or puff)
$\frac{1}{2}$ pint white sauce
1 lb cod
6 oz sweet corn
1 oz grated Cheddar cheese

1. Thaw pastry 1–2 hours at room temperature.
2. Thaw white sauce by gently heating through in pan.
3. Use cod, sweet corn and cheese from frozen.

FROM THE STORECUPBOARD

Salt and pepper
1 egg, beaten

4. Poach cod for about 20 minutes, drain and flake.
5. Mix fish with sweet corn, seasoning and sauce.
6. Line $8\frac{1}{2}$ inch pie dish with 2/3rd pastry and pile in filling.
7. Cover with remaining pastry.
8. Brush with beaten egg and sprinkle with cheese.
9. Bake in fairly hot oven until golden.

Note
1. May be cooked, cooled and frozen.
2. Storage time in freezer: 4–6 weeks.

COD WITH GRAPES

Serves 4

Cooking Time: 25–30 minutes

FROM THE FREEZER

4 cod fillets

1. Use cod from frozen.

FROM THE STORECUPBOARD

$\frac{1}{2}$ pint milk
Salt
Peppercorns
1 blade mace
1 lemon
3–4 oz grapes, halved and de-seeded
$\frac{1}{2}$ oz butter
$\frac{1}{2}$ oz flour
1 egg yolk

2. Add salt, a few peppercorns, mace and juice of half the lemon to milk, and bring gently to boil.
3. Place cod and half grapes in shallow pan, and poach in flavoured milk.
4. Allow up to 30 minutes for thick steaks; if thawed, 10–15 minutes according to thickness.
5. Remove fish to serving dish and keep warm. Strain milk.
6. Melt butter, add flour and cook for 1 minute. Blend in milk and cook, stirring to thicken.
7. Remove sauce from heat and beat in egg yolk.
8. Pour over fish and garnish with remaining grapes and lemon slices.

Note

1. May be cooked, cooled and frozen. Reserve garnish until serving.
2. Storage time in freezer: 4–6 weeks.

KIPPER CHEESE TWISTS

Makes 20 to 25

Cooking Time: 15 minutes
Temperature: Gas No. 7 or 425°F (218°C)

FROM THE FREEZER

8 oz packet kipper fillets
7½ oz packet puff pastry

1. Thaw kipper fillets and pastry 2–3 hours at room temperature.

FROM THE STORECUPBOARD

1 egg, beaten
1 oz grated Parmesan cheese

2. Cook kipper fillets as directed on packet.
3. Remove skin and pound fillets.
4. Roll out pastry very thinly. Cut into 2 oblong strips.
5. Brush 1 piece with egg, cover with mashed kipper to within ½ inch of edges, and cover with second strip of pastry.
6. Seal edges well, and cut into ½ inch fingers across pastry.
7. Brush with egg and sprinkle with cheese.
8. Twist each finger several times and place on greased baking sheet.
9. Bake in hot oven.
10. Serve hot or cold.

Note

1. May be prepared and frozen for subsequent baking (see page 33 for pastry details) or may be baked, cooled and frozen.
2. Storage time in freezer: uncooked, 4–6 weeks; cooked, 2–3 months.

KIPPER STAR PIE

Serves 8

Cooking Time: 35 minutes
Temperature: Gas No. 7 or 425°F (218°C)

FROM THE FREEZER

2 (7½ oz) packets shortcrust pastry
8 kippers, on the bone

1. Thaw pastry and kippers at room temperature 2–3 hours.

FROM THE STORECUPBOARD

8 spring onions, chopped
2 tomatoes, skinned
1 lemon
1 tablespoon chopped parsley
1 egg, beaten

2. Roll out each packet of pastry thinly into largest possible circle.
3. Skin and bone kippers, keeping tails intact.
4. Place 1 chopped spring onion and ¼ tomato, sliced, on each kipper, and fold over in half.
5. Squeeze lemon juice and sprinkle a little chopped parsley on each kipper.
6. Place kippers in star fashion on 1 circle of pastry with tails extending slightly over edges of circle. Brush with beaten egg between kippers.
7. Cover with second piece of pastry, sealing edges well.
8. Brush top with egg and bake in hot oven.
9. Serve hot or cold.

Note

1. May be cooked, cooled and frozen, but best eaten fresh.
2. Storage time in freezer: 2–3 months.

KIPPER COCKTAIL

Serves 4

Cooking Time: None

FROM THE FREEZER

8 oz packet kipper fillets
2 tablespoons orange juice, undiluted
4–5 oz cream

1. Thaw kippers 2–3 hours at room temperature.
2. Thaw juice and cream about 2 hours at room temperature.

FROM THE STORECUPBOARD

1 tablespoon lemon juice
½ bunch watercress, finely chopped
1 lettuce
Slices of lemon and parsley sprigs

3. Place kippers in shallow dish. Pour on lemon and orange juice and marinate for 12 hours in refrigerator.
4. Drain, keeping 1 tablespoon of marinade, and cut kippers into ½ inch wide strips.
5. Whip cream and stir in tablespoon of marinade and finely chopped watercress.
6. Shred lettuce and place in bottom of 4 glasses.
7. Top with kippers and cover with cream mixture.
8. Garnish each glass with twisted slice of lemon and parsley sprig.

KIPPER KEDGEREE

Serves 4

Cooking Time: 20–30 minutes
Temperature: Gas No. 3 or 325°F (163°C)

FROM THE FREEZER

8 oz packet kipper fillets
4–5 oz cream
Chopped parsley

1. Thaw kippers 2–3 hours at room temperature.
2. Thaw cream about 2 hours at room temperature.
3. Use parsley from frozen.

FROM THE STORECUPBOARD

½ lb long grain rice.
4 hard-boiled eggs
2 oz butter
Salt and pepper

4. Boil rice for 10 minutes in plenty of fast-boiling salted water.
5. Drain and rinse.
6. Cook kippers by standing in jug of boiling water for 5 minutes.
7. Skin and flake kippers.
8. Shell and chop eggs.
9. Melt butter, and add flaked kipper and chopped eggs.
10. Stir in rice, cream, and salt and pepper.
11. Place in 2½ pint ovenproof dish, cover and heat through in warm oven.
12. Serve at once sprinkled with chopped parsley.

Note

1. Unsuitable for freezing as hard-boiled eggs will become leathery.

KIPPER PÂTÉ

Serves 4 to 6

Cooking Time: None

FROM THE FREEZER

8 oz packet kipper fillets

1. Thaw kippers 2–3 hours at room temperature.

FROM THE STORECUPBOARD

6 oz butter
2 tablespoons lemon juice
1 clove garlic, crushed (optional)
Black pepper

2. Cover thawed kippers with boiling water and allow to stand for 5 minutes.
3. Skin and remove bones.
4. Pound flesh with wooden spoon and blend well with softened butter.
5. Add lemon juice and garlic. Season to taste.
6. Pile into straight-sided serving pot.
7. Serve with thin slices of hot buttered toast.

Note

1. Made-up pâté freezes well. It takes about 3–4 hours at room temperature to thaw.
2. Storage time in freezer: 1–2 months.

INDIAN SOLE KNOTS

Serves 4

Cooking Time: Approximately 15 minutes

FROM THE FREEZER

4 fillets of sole
4–5 oz cream

1. Thaw sole and cream about 2 hours at room temperature.

FROM THE STORECUPBOARD

2 dessert apples
4 tomatoes
$\frac{1}{4}$ pint milk
2 oz butter
1 large onion, chopped
1 level tablespoon curry powder
Salt and pepper
Lemon wedges and chopped parsley for garnish

2. Peel, core and chop apples.
3. Skin, seed and chop tomatoes.
4. Add milk to cream.
5. Skin each fillet and cut into 4 long thin strips.
6. Tie each strip into a single knot.
7. Fry onion in butter until transparent. Add curry powder and fry for 1 minute.
8. Add apples and tomatoes and fry for 5 minutes.
9. Add cream mixture and bring gently to boil. Season.
10. Add sole knots and simmer for 8–10 minutes.
11. Serve with boiled rice and garnish with lemon wedges and chopped parsley.

Note

1. Large fillets of plaice may be used instead of sole.
2. Whole dish may be cooked and frozen. Completely thaw before gently reheating.
3. Storage time in freezer: 4–6 weeks.

PLAICE OR SOLE WITH YOGURT SAUCE

Serves 4

Cooking Time: 30 minutes
Temperature: Gas No. 4 or 350°F (177°C)

FROM THE FREEZER

5 oz carton plain yogurt
4 large fillets of sole or 8 small fillets plaice
Handful sultana grapes

1. Thaw yogurt and fillets approximately 1 hour at room temperature.
2. Use grapes from frozen.

FROM THE STORECUPBOARD

2–3 tablespoons mayonnaise
1 teaspoon lemon juice
$\frac{1}{4}$ level teaspoon curry powder
1 oz butter
4 oz button mushrooms

3. Mix together mayonnaise, lemon juice, curry powder and yogurt.
4. Butter shallow 2 pint ovenproof dish.
5. Spread some of sauce mixture on to fillets and roll up.
6. Stand them in dish and pour over remaining sauce.
7. Cook mushrooms and grapes in butter for 1 minute.
8. Add to fish.
9. Cover with lid or foil.
10. Bake in moderate oven.

Note

1. Unsuitable for freezing as sauce tends to separate.

MARSALA PLAICE

Serves 4

Cooking Time: 15 minutes

FROM THE FREEZER

4 fillets of plaice
Parsley butter

1. Thaw plaice 25–30 minutes at room temperature.
2. Use parsley butter from frozen.

FROM THE STORECUPBOARD

1 oz flour
Salt and pepper
3 oz butter
2 fluid oz marsala wine

3. Coat fillets in seasoned flour.
4. Melt butter over moderate heat. Add fillets and cook until golden brown on 1 side.
5. Add marsala, turn fish, and cook on other side.
6. Lift on to warmed serving dish. Pour over pan liquors.
7. Serve with parsley butter and crisp green salad.

Note

1. Parsley and other savoury butter (see page 30).

PLAICE FLORENTINE

Serves 4

Cooking Time: 10–15 minutes
Temperature: Gas No. 5 or 375°F (191°C)

FROM THE FREEZER

8 small fillets of plaice
½ pint thick white sauce
12 oz sieved spinach
4 oz grated Cheddar cheese

1. Thaw plaice 25–30 minutes at room temperature.
2. Heat sauce through gently from frozen.
3. Use spinach and cheese from frozen.

FROM THE STORECUPBOARD

Salt and pepper
4 tablespoons white wine
1 teaspoon Worcestershire sauce

4. Season fish and roll into compact parcel with skin side inside.

5. Place fish in buttered $2\frac{1}{2}$ pint shallow ovenproof dish. Add wine and cover with lid or foil.
6. Bake in fairly hot oven.
7. Cook spinach as directed on packet.
8. Remove fish and keep warm.
9. Add fish liquor, Worcestershire sauce and half the cheese to white sauce.
10. Place spinach on base of dish, top with fish, pour sauce over and sprinkle with remaining cheese.
11. Brown in hot oven or under grill until cheese is bubbly and brown.

Note

1. Whole dish may be prepared up to and including stage 10, cooled and frozen in deep foil container.
2. Reheat in moderate oven.
3. Storage time in freezer: 4–6 weeks.

SMOKED FISH SLICE

Serves 6

Cooking Time: 25 minutes
Temperature: Gas No. 7 or 425°F (218°C)

FROM THE FREEZER

$13\frac{1}{2}$ oz packet puff pastry
1 lb smoked haddock

1. Thaw pastry 1–2 hours at room temperature.
2. Use haddock from frozen.

FROM THE STORECUPBOARD

4 hard-boiled eggs, chopped
1 tablespoon parsley, chopped
1 tablespoon lemon juice
Salt and pepper
1 egg, beaten

3. Poach haddock gently in a little milk or water. Drain and flake.
4. Roll out pastry thinly to a rectangle, about 12 by 14 inches.
5. Make 3 inch cuts at 1 inch intervals along both 14 inch sides of pastry.
6. Combine cooked fish, hard-boiled eggs, parsley, lemon juice and seasoning.
7. Place filling down centre of pastry.
8. Brush cut sides of pastry with beaten egg. Fold strips over filling

alternately from each side.
9. Brush slice with beaten egg.
10. Bake in hot oven.
11. Serve hot or cold.

SMOKED HADDOCK OMELET

Serves 1

Cooking Time: Approximately 5–6 minutes

FROM THE FREEZER

3 oz smoked haddock
2 tablespoons cream

1. Thaw haddock and cream about 1 hour at room temperature.

FROM THE STORECUPBOARD

3 eggs
3 teaspoons cold water
Salt and pepper
$\frac{1}{2}$ oz butter

2. Poach haddock gently in a little milk or water for about 2–3 minutes. Flake and combine with cream. Keep warm.
3. Beat eggs, water and seasonings together in basin with fork until blended.
4. Melt butter in 7 inch omelet pan, getting pan very hot but not allowing butter to brown.
5. Pour in egg mixture and pull sides of omelet into centre of pan with fork or spatula. Egg sets as soon as it meets hot pan surface. Immediately move this cooked egg around in pan, allowing liquid egg to meet pan surface and cook.
6. Continue in this way, working very quickly until there is no liquid egg on top of omelet, although it should still be quite moist.
7. Add prepared filling on to the half of omelet opposite handle of pan.
8. Flick over other half and just allow to seal over heat for a few moments.
9. Tip omelet on to serving plate and serve at once.

Note

1. Omelets do not reheat well if cooked frozen.
2. For freezing of small quantities of cream (see page 29).

ORANGY TROUT

Serves 4

Cooking Time: Approximately 25 minutes

FROM THE FREEZER

4 tablespoons orange juice
4 trout

1. Thaw orange juice about 30 minutes at room temperature.
2. Use trout from frozen.

FROM THE STORECUPBOARD

½ pint fish stock or water
4 tablespoons lemon juice
2 oz butter
2 level tablespoons arrowroot
1 tablespoon parsley, chopped
Slices of orange and lemon for garnish

3. Bring stock to boil.
4. Place trout in stock and poach gently for about 20 minutes.
5. Remove trout from stock and keep warm.
6. Strain stock, and add to lemon and orange juice.
7. Melt butter in pan and stir in arrowroot. Gradually add stock and juice mixture.
8. Bring to boil, stirring all the time.
9. Add chopped parsley.
10. Serve with sauce poured over trout.
11. Garnish with slices of orange and lemon.

Note

1. Fish stock can be made up in quantity from fish bones and skin, etc, and frozen in ½ pints.

PRAWN AND GRAPEFRUIT SALAD

Serves 4

Cooking Time: None

FROM THE FREEZER

4 oz prawns

1. Thaw prawns about 1 hour at room temperature.

FROM THE STORECUPBOARD

2 grapefruit
¼ cucumber, finely chopped
3 tablespoons French dressing

2. Cut each grapefruit in half and remove segments.
3. Mix grapefruit segments, cucumber and prawns together with French dressing.
4. Place in grapefruit shells. Chill before serving.

Note

1. Well drained canned grapefruit segments may be used. Pile mixture into frozen grapefruit shells straight from freezer.

DRUNKEN PRAWNS

Serves 4

Cooking Time: 10–15 minutes

FROM THE FREEZER

1 lb prawns
4–5 oz cream

1. Thaw prawns and cream about 2 hours at room temperature.

FROM THE STORECUPBOARD

2 oz butter
2 tablespoons olive oil
1 medium onion, chopped
1 clove garlic, crushed
2 tomatoes, skinned, seeded and chopped
Salt and pepper
6 tablespoons whisky
6 tablespoons dry white wine
1 level teaspoon cornflour
¼ level teaspoon dried tarragon
1 egg yolk, beaten

2. Heat butter and oil, and fry onion and garlic.
3. Add tomatoes and prawns. Season to taste.
4. Pour over 4 tablespoons of whisky, ignite with match and allow to flame for a second or two. Extinguish by pouring on wine.
5. Simmer for 5 minutes.
6. Remove prawns from pan and keep warm. Blend cornflour, remaining

whisky and cream together.

7. Add to sauce and beat well while bringing to boil.
8. Boil for 1 minute and remove from heat.
9. Add tarragon and beaten egg yolk.
10. Pour sauce over prawns and serve immediately on bed of plain boiled rice.

PRAWN PUFFS

Serves 4

Cooking time: 4–6 minutes deep fry

FROM THE FREEZER

1 lb prawns, king size
7½ oz puff pastry

1. Thaw prawns and pastry about 1 hour at room temperature.

FROM THE STORECUPBOARD

1 egg, beaten
Lemon wedges and parsley sprigs

2. Roll out pastry very thinly.
3. Cut pastry into rounds a little less in diameter than the prawns.
4. Brush each piece of pastry with egg and wrap around each king size prawn so that a little prawn sticks out at either end.
5. Deep fry for 4–6 minutes until puffed and golden. Drain on absorbent kitchen paper.
6. Serve with lemon wedges and parsley sprigs.

PRAWN BITES

Serves 4

Cooking Time: 3–4 minutes deep fry

FROM THE FREEZER

4 oz prawns
1 lb cod
4–5 oz cream

1. Thaw prawns, cod and cream about 2 hours at room temperature.

FROM THE STORECUPBOARD

3 tablespoons lemon juice
1 tablespoon anchovy essence
Salt and pepper
5 oz self-raising flour
¼ pint thick mayonnaise
1 teaspoon Worcestershire sauce
1 tablespoon tomato ketchup

2. Flake raw cod with sharp knife.
3. Add chopped prawns.
4. Add 2 tablespoons lemon juice, anchovy essence, salt and pepper.
5. Add flour and mix well.
6. Drop in teaspoonfuls into hot fat and fry for 3–4 minutes until golden brown.
7. Drain on absorbent kitchen paper.
8. Serve on cocktail sticks with party dip.

Note

1. To make dip combine cream (whipped), ¼ pint thick mayonnaise, 1 tablespoon lemon juice, 1 teaspoon Worcestershire sauce and 1 tablespoon tomato ketchup.

PRAWN STUFFED AVOCADOS

Serves 4

Cooking Time: None

FROM THE FREEZER

4–6 oz prawns
2 tablespoons cream

1. Thaw prawns and cream about 2 hours at room temperature.

FROM THE STORECUPBOARD

2 large avocado pears
Lemon juice
2 tablespoons thick mayonnaise
Pinch cayenne
Salt and pepper
Lettuce leaves

2. Cut avocados in half, remove stone and sprinkle with lemon juice to prevent discolouration.
3. Mix together mayonnaise, whipped cream and seasonings.
4. Fold in prawns.
5. Pile mixture into avocados and serve chilled on lettuce leaves.

Note

1. Freezing of small quantities of cream (see page 29).

MELON AND PRAWN COCKTAIL

Serves 8 to 10

Cooking Time: None

FROM THE FREEZER

1 lb melon balls
½ pint cream
½ lb prawns

1. Thaw melon balls 3–4 hours at room temperature.
2. Thaw cream about 2 hours at room temperature.
3. Thaw prawns 1 hour at room temperature.

FROM THE STORECUPBOARD

1 green pepper or ½ cucumber, diced
2 tablespoons lemon juice
Lemon slices and parsley sprigs

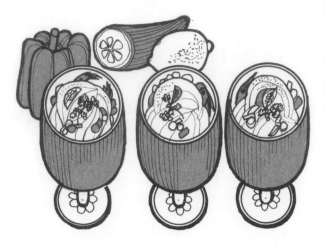

4. Strain away a little of melon syrup.
5. Combine melon balls, diced pepper and prawns.
6. Pile into wine or sundae glasses.
7. Add lemon juice to whipped cream.
8. Pour over melon and prawn mixture.
9. Serve garnished with twist of sliced lemon and parsley sprig.

Note

1. Alternatively pile mixture into 2 whole melon shells straight from freezer.

CRAB TART

Serves 4 to 6

Cooking Time: 30 minutes
Temperature: Gas No. 4 or 350°F (177°C)

FROM THE FREEZER

½ lb crab meat
4–5 oz cream
8 inch pastry flan case, baked blind

1. Thaw crab meat and cream about 2 hours at room temperature.
2. Use flan case from frozen.

FROM THE STORECUPBOARD

1 oz butter
2 tablespoons parsley, chopped
2 tablespoons sherry
3 egg yolks
¼ pint milk
Salt and pepper
Grated nutmeg

3. Cook crab meat and parsley in butter.

4. Add sherry and turn mixture into flan case.
5. Whisk egg yolks. Add cream and milk, and whisk until thick and creamy.
6. Add seasoning and nutmeg, and pour over crab meat in flan case.
7. Bake in moderate oven.
8. Serve hot or cold.

Note

1. Using fresh crab, flan may be cooked, cooled and frozen.
2. Storage time in freezer: 4—6 weeks.

DEVILLED CRAB

Serves 4

Cooking Time: 20 minutes
Temperature: Gas No. 7 or 425°F (218°C)

FROM THE FREEZER

1 lb crab meat
3 tablespoons grated Cheddar cheese
2 oz white roux (see page 30)

1. Thaw crab meat about 2 hours at room temperature.
2. Use cheese and roux from frozen.

FROM THE STORECUPBOARD

¼ pint milk
1 teaspoon made mustard
2 tablespoons Worcestershire sauce
2 tablespoons parsley, chopped
1 tablespoon onion, chopped
1 tablespoon green pepper
Salt and pepper (freshly ground black, if possible)
4 hard-boiled eggs

3. Add frozen roux to cold milk and bring to boil stirring to thicken.
4. Add mustard, Worcestershire sauce, parsley, onion, green pepper, salt and pepper.
5. Chop eggs and flake crab meat. Add to sauce stirring gently so as not to break up too much.
6. Fill 4 dishes with mixture and sprinkle cheese on top.
7. Bake in hot oven.
8. Serve hot with brown bread and butter.

SEAFOOD CASSEROLE

Serves 6

Cooking Time: 30 minutes
Temperature: Gas No. 4 or 350°F (177°C)

FROM THE FREEZER

1 lb white crab meat
4—6 oz prawns
2 oz grated Cheddar cheese

1. Thaw crab for 2 hours at room temperature.
2. Use prawns and cheese from frozen.

FROM THE STORECUPBOARD

½ lb shell pasta
15 oz can lobster soup
1 tablespoon lemon juice
1 level teaspoon celery salt
1 teaspoon Soy sauce
4 oz button mushrooms
½ oz butter

3. Barely cook (about 8 minutes) pasta in plenty of boiling salted water.
4. Drain pasta and place in buttered ovenproof dish.
5. Add lemon juice, celery salt, Soy sauce and mushrooms to soup, and heat through.
6. Stir flaked crab meat and prawns carefully into soup mixture.
7. Pour over pasta.
8. Cover with grated cheese.
9. Bake, uncovered, in moderate oven until bubbly brown on top.

Note

1. Any combination of shellfish may be used: crab, lobster, crawfish, prawns, shrimps, scallops.
2. To freeze completed dish, cook pasta as above. Use fresh crab or other shellfish. Add cold soup with mushrooms and seasonings, and prawns straight from freezer. Pour over pasta, pack and freeze immediately.
3. Allow to thaw 4—5 hours in refrigerator. Cover with grated cheese and bake as above.
4. Storage time in freezer: 4—6 weeks.

CRAB PÂTÉ

Serves 8

Cooking Time: 20 minutes

FROM THE FREEZER

1 lb dressed crab (brown and white meat)
1 tablespoon cream

1. Thaw crab 1–2 hours at room temperature.
2. Thaw cream about 30 minutes at room temperature.

FROM THE STORECUPBOARD

1 tablespoon milk
4 egg yolks
4 oz butter
$\frac{1}{4}$ level teaspoon cayenne
2 tablespoons brandy or sherry.

3. Mix together double cream, milk and egg yolks.
4. Melt butter and cook crab meat. Remove from heat.

5. Add cream and egg mixture, and stir carefully over low heat for about 10 minutes to thicken.
6. Remove from heat. Add cayenne and brandy.
7. Fill individual buttered dishes and chill.
8. Serve with hot buttered toast.

Note

1. For freezing of small quantities of cream (see page 29).
2. May be cooked, cooled and frozen.
3. Storage life in freezer: 4–6 weeks.

CRAB BISQUE

Serves 4

Cooking Time: 10–15 minutes

FROM THE FREEZER

$\frac{1}{2}$ lb brown crab meat
1 pint white sauce
4–5 oz cream
Parsley
Croûtons

1. Thaw crab, sauce and cream about 2 hours at room temperature.
2. Use parsley and croûtons from frozen.

FROM THE STORECUPBOARD

1 oz butter
Salt and pepper
2 tablespoons lemon juice
1 tablespoon Worcestershire sauce
1 level teaspoon dry mustard
1 glass sherry

3. Melt butter. Add crab, salt, pepper, lemon juice, Worcestershire sauce and mustard.
4. Combine with white sauce and simmer for 10–15 minutes.
5. Sieve or liquidize.
6. Add sherry and half the cream.
7. Garnish with remainder of cream, chopped parsley and croûtons.
8. Serve very hot or cold.

Note

1. Useful way of using brown crab meat in 1 lb packet of frozen dressed crab.
2. Cooked dish may be frozen, but as quick to prepare as above.
3. Croûtons freeze well.

CRAB AND ARTICHOKE BAKE

Serves 4

Cooking Time: 40 minutes
Temperature: Gas No. 5 or 375°F
(191°C)

FROM THE FREEZER

12 oz crab meat
½ pint thick white sauce
4–5 oz cream
2 oz grated Cheddar cheese

1. Thaw crab meat, white sauce and cream about 2 hours at room temperature.
2. Use cheese from frozen.

FROM THE STORECUPBOARD

14 oz can artichoke hearts, drained
1 oz butter
½ lb mushrooms
1 tablespoon Worcestershire sauce
2 tablespoons sherry
Salt and pepper

3. Place artichoke hearts in buttered 2 pint shallow casserole dish.
4. Put butter in frying pan and fry mushrooms gently.
5. Add cream, Worcestershire sauce, sherry and seasonings to white sauce.
6. Flake crab meat over artichokes.
7. Top with mushrooms, sauce and cheese.
8. Bake, uncovered, in fairly hot oven until bubbly and brown.

Note

1. If fresh crab, etc, is used, dish may be prepared up to stage 7, cooled and frozen.
2. Thaw before baking as above.
3. Storage time in freezer: 4–6 weeks.

QUICK CRAWFISH THERMIDOR

Serves 4 or 8 for starters

Cooking Time: 2–3 minutes under a hot grill

FROM THE FREEZER

8 crawfish tails
4–5 oz cream
2 oz white roux

1. Thaw crawfish tails overnight in refrigerator or several hours at room temperature.
2. Thaw cream about 2 hours at room temperature.

FROM THE STORECUPBOARD

Small piece lemon
½ pint milk
4 tablespoons sherry
Pinch cayenne
½ teaspoon made mustard
1 teaspoon Worcestershire sauce
Salt and pepper
Parmesan cheese
Chopped parsley

3. Place crawfish tails in cold salted water with a little piece of lemon.
4. Bring to boil and simmer for 1 minute.
5. Remove pan from heat. Leave tails in water for about 5 minutes.
6. Cut crawfish tails in half lengthways and carefully remove meat from shell.
7. Cut flesh into bite-size pieces.
8. Make thick white sauce from roux and milk.
9. Add sherry, cayenne, mustard and Worcestershire sauce. Add cream and season to taste.
10. Add diced crawfish to sauce and gently heat through.
11. Spoon into crawfish shells, sprinkle with Parmesan cheese and brown under hot grill.
12. Serve sprinkled with chopped parsley.

Note

1. For starters, serve 2 half shells per person.
2. For main course, allow 2 whole crawfish tails per person and serve out of shells with plain boiled rice.

SHRIMP BLINTZES

Serves 4 for starters

Cooking Time: 5 minutes deep fry

FROM THE FREEZER

12 small thin pancakes
2 (2 oz) cartons potted shrimps
2 oz breadcrumbs

1. Thaw pancakes and shrimps about 1 hour at room temperature.
2. Thaw breadcrumbs ½ hour at room temperature.

FROM THE STORECUPBOARD

1 egg beaten with 2 tablespoons milk

3. Place spoonful of shrimps in one quarter of pancake.
4. Fold in half, then half again to form triangle.
5. Dip stuffed pancake in beaten egg and milk.
6. Coat with breadcrumbs.
7. Deep fry until crisp and golden brown.
8. Repeat this method with remainder of pancakes.
9. Serve hot with Tartare sauce.

Note

1. If freshly made pancakes and filling are used, they may be prepared up to frying stage and frozen.
2. Allow to thaw completely before frying.
3. Storage time in freezer: 4—6 weeks.

PLAT DE FRUITS DE MER

Serves 8 to 10

Cooking Time: Approximately 10—15 minutes for smoked haddock and crawfish tails

FROM THE FREEZER

8 oz packet kipper fillets
8 oz prawns
1 lb dressed crab (brown and white meat)
½ lb smoked haddock
8 crawfish tails
6½ oz carton orange juice
4—5 oz cream

1. Thaw all ingredients except cream 3—4 hours at room temperature or overnight in refrigerator.
2. Thaw cream about 2 hours at room temperature.

FROM THE STORECUPBOARD

1 tablespoon lemon juice
2 tablespoons mayonnaise
1 teaspoon wine vinegar
Pinch mustard
Rice Salad (see page 70), double quantities
Anchovy fillets
Black olives

3. Marinate kipper fillets (see Kipper Cocktail, page 56).
4. Toss white crab meat in mayonnaise.
5. Blend teaspoon of vinegar and pinch of mustard with brown crab meat.
6. Poach and cool smoked haddock, then flake and toss in cream to which a little lemon juice has been added.
7. Cook crawfish tails (see page 65) and cut in half.
8. Choose large oval or round platter, or cover tray with foil.
9. Pile Rice Salad in centre and garnish with strips of anchovy fillets and black olives.
10. Surround with scallop shells filled with fish prepared as above. Place crawfish tails between each shell.

SCAMPI WITH PINEAPPLE

Serves 4

Cooking Time: Approximately 5 minutes

FROM THE FREEZER

1 lb jumbo scampi

1. Thaw scampi about 1 hour at room temperature.

FROM THE STORECUPBOARD

12 oz can pineapple chunks
1 level tablespoon cornflour
¼ level teaspoon ground ginger
1 tablespoon honey
1 tablespoon wine vinegar
4 oz bottle pineapple juice
2 tablespoons Soy sauce

2. Strain juice from can of pineapple.
3. Blend cornflour with a little of the juice to smooth paste.
4. Add remaining juice, ground ginger, honey, wine vinegar, bottled pineapple juice and Soy sauce. Gently bring to boil, stirring all the time.

5. Place scampi and pineapple alternately on skewers.
6. Dip filled skewers in sauce.
7. Place under moderate grill until lightly browned all over.
8. Serve on bed of Rice Salad (see page 70).

Vegetables

ASPARAGUS POLONAISE

Serves 3

Cooking Time: 10–15 minutes

FROM THE FREEZER
12 oz asparagus spears
1 oz breadcrumbs

1. Use asparagus and breadcrumbs from frozen.

FROM THE STORECUPBOARD
2 oz butter
1 hard-boiled egg, finely chopped
1 teaspoon parsley, chopped
Salt and pepper

2. Cook asparagus as directed on packet and lay in serving dish.
3. Melt butter. Add breadcrumbs and fry until golden.
4. Stir in finely chopped hard-boiled egg, parsley and seasonings.
5. Pour over asparagus and serve.

BROAD BEANS WITH YOGURT

Serves 4

Cooking time: 10–15 minutes

FROM THE FREEZER
1 carton plain yogurt
12 oz broad beans

1. Thaw yogurt about 2 hours at room temperature.
2. Use broad beans from frozen.

FROM THE STORECUPBOARD
2 tablespoons long grain rice
1 clove garlic, crushed
Salt and pepper
1 egg, beaten

3. Cook beans as directed on packet. Cook rice in boiling salted water for 10 minutes. Strain beans and rice and mix together while still hot.
4. Stir garlic into yogurt.
5. Add salt, pepper and yogurt to beans and rice, and heat through gently.
6. Add beaten egg and stir over a low heat until sauce thickens.
7. Serve hot or cold.

67

PAPRIKA BEANS

Serves 4

Cooking Time: 15–20 minutes

FROM THE FREEZER

4–5 oz cream
1 lb French beans

1. Thaw cream about 2 hours at room temperature.
2. Use beans from frozen.

FROM THE STORECUPBOARD

2 oz butter
1 large onion, finely chopped
1 level tablespoon paprika
2 level tablespoons flour
Salt and pepper

3. Cook beans in boiling salted water until only just tender. Strain.
4. Melt butter and fry onion gently until transparent.
5. Remove from heat and add paprika.
6. Blend flour with cream and add to onion mixture, stirring all the time.
7. Cook on low heat for about 5 minutes.
8. Add beans, and salt and pepper, simmer for 5 minutes and serve.

SPINACH SOUP

Serves 6

Cooking Time: 15–20 minutes

FROM THE FREEZER

4–5 oz cream
9 oz packet spinach
1 pint very strong chicken stock

1. Thaw cream about 2 hours at room temperature.
2. Use spinach and stock from frozen.

FROM THE STORECUPBOARD

2 pints water
1 oz butter
1 oz flour
Salt and pepper
Pinch nutmeg
1 egg yolk

3. Cook spinach as directed on packet. Drain well.
4. Place frozen stock in pan with water and bring slowly to boil.
5. Melt butter, stir in flour and cook for 1 minute.

6. Add stock gradually, stirring all the time.
7. Add drained and chopped spinach. Simmer for 15 minutes over low heat.
8. Season with salt, pepper and nutmeg.
9. Blend egg yolk and cream together in base of soup tureen.
10. Add hot soup, stirring all the time, and serve.

Note

1. This becomes a meal in itself if served with Cheese Bread (see page 94).

FRENCH STYLE PEAS

Serves 4

Cooking Time: 30 minutes

FROM THE FREEZER

12 oz peas

1. Use peas from frozen.

FROM THE STORECUPBOARD

Lettuce leaves
1 small onion or 2 shallots or spring onions, chopped
1 oz butter
1 teaspoon sugar
Salt and pepper

2. Put several washed lettuce leaves into thick pan.
3. Add onions or shallots and peas.
4. Add butter, sugar and seasonings, and cover with more lettuce leaves.
5. Cook slowly for about 30 minutes.

Note

1. If oven is in use, prepare as above and cook in covered ovenproof dish, allowing extra 10–15 minutes cooking time.

GREEN PEA SOUP

Serves 4

Cooking Time: 5–10 minutes.

FROM THE FREEZER

10 oz peas
2 (1 oz) roux packs (see page 30)

4 chopped mint cubes (see page 26)

1. Use peas, roux and mint from frozen.

FROM THE STORECUPBOARD

1 level teaspoon sugar
2 tablespoons cream
1 pint milk
Salt and pepper

2. Cook peas with sugar and mint cubes in $\frac{1}{4}$ pint of water for 5–6 minutes.
3. Make sauce by placing roux in milk and bringing to boil, stirring until thickened.
4. Purée peas with minted water in sieve or liquidizer.
5. Stir purée into white sauce with 1 tablespoon cream.
6. Check seasoning. Bring carefully to boil.
7. Pour soup into heated tureen.
8. Trickle second spoonful of cream into centre for decoration.
9. Serve hot or chilled.

BABY ONION FLAN

Serves 4

Cooking Time: 30–35 minutes
Temperature: Gas No. 5 or 375°F (191°C)

FROM THE FREEZER

8 inch baked shortcrust pastry flan case
8 oz packet onions in white sauce
1 oz grated Cheddar cheese

1. Use pastry case, onions and cheese from frozen.

FROM THE STORECUPBOARD
2 eggs

2. Place flan case on baking tray.
3. Cook onions in sauce as directed on packet.
4. Beat eggs and stir in onion mix.
5. Pour mixture into flan case.
6. Sprinkle with grated cheese.
7. Bake in fairly hot oven.
8. Serve hot.

RICE SALAD

Serves 4

Cooking Time: Approximately 15 minutes

FROM THE FREEZER

8 oz mixed vegetables

1. Use vegetables from frozen.

FROM THE STORECUPBOARD

4 oz long grain rice
1 chicken stock cube
½ pint water
4 tablespoons mayonnaise or French dressing

2. Cook rice in plenty of salted water until barely cooked, about 8–9 minutes.
3. Drain.
4. Dissolve chicken stock cube in water, and then add vegetables and rice.
5. Simmer until vegetables are cooked.
6. Drain if necessary and allow to cool.
7. Mix with mayonnaise or French dressing.
8. Chill before serving.

Note

1. Rice which has been cooked and frozen can be used straight from freezer, simmered with mixed vegetables in stock.

CAULIFLOWER AU GRATIN

Serves 4

Cooking Time: 10–15 minutes

FROM THE FREEZER

1 lb cauliflower florets
1 oz grated Cheddar cheese
1 oz white breadcrumbs

1. Use cauliflower, cheese and breadcrumbs from frozen.

FROM THE STORECUPBOARD

½ pint milk
4 hard-boiled eggs, chopped

1 packet onion sauce mix
Salt and pepper

2. Cook cauliflower gently in milk for about 10 minutes.
3. Drain and place in buttered 2 pint ovenproof dish with hard-boiled eggs.
4. Use milk to make up packet sauce mix.
5. Pour over cauliflower.
6. Mix cheese, breadcrumbs and seasoning together.
7. Sprinkle over cauliflower and brown under grill.

SPROUTS IN BATTER

Serves 4

Cooking Time: 10 minutes deep fry

FROM THE FREEZER

1 lb sprouts
1 oz grated Cheddar cheese

1. Thaw sprouts about 30 minutes at room temperature.
2. Use cheese from frozen.

FROM THE STORECUPBOARD

2 oz flour
Pinch salt
2 teaspoons salad oil
1 egg, separated
About ⅛ pint warm water
Salt and pepper

3. Sift flour and salt into bowl, and make well in middle.
4. Add oil and egg yolk, and mix all to coating batter with warm water.
5. Beat until light and then put in a cold place for about 1 hour.
6. Just before using, whisk egg white until just stiff and fold into batter.
7. Season sprouts and dip in batter. Deep fry for 10 minutes, until coating is crisp and golden.
8. Serve with grated cheese sprinkled on top.

Note

1. Mushrooms, asparagus and cauliflower can also be cooked in batter, using this method to achieve a light and crispy batter.

SWEET CORN CUSTARD

Serves 4

Cooking Time: 1 hour
Temperature: Gas No. 3 or 325°F (163°C)

FROM THE FREEZER

6 oz sweet corn
3 oz grated Cheddar cheese

1. Use sweet corn and cheese from frozen.

FROM THE STORECUPBOARD

3 eggs
1 pint milk
Salt and pepper

2. Place sweet corn in buttered 2 pint ovenproof dish.
3. Beat eggs well with a little milk.
4. Add remaining milk, half the cheese and seasoning.
5. Pour custard over sweet corn. Top with remaining cheese.
6. Bake slowly in warm oven.

SWEET CORN SALAD

Serves 5 to 6

Cooking Time: 5–10 minutes

FROM THE FREEZER

12 oz sweet corn

1. Use sweet corn from frozen.

FROM THE STORECUPBOARD

8 oz button mushrooms, sliced
2 tablespoons olive oil
1 tablespoon lemon juice
1 teaspoon chopped parsley
1 teaspoon chopped chives
French dressing

2. Cook sweet corn in minimum of salted water for 5–6 minutes.
3. Drain and leave to cool.
4. Cook mushrooms over low heat in oil and lemon juice for 2–3 minutes.
5. Mix together sweet corn, mushrooms, parsley and chives.
6. Toss in French dressing and serve.

Fruit

ORANGE SORBET

Serves 6

Cooking Time: None

FROM THE FREEZER

6¼ oz can orange juice, undiluted

1. Use juice from frozen.

FROM THE STORECUPBOARD

6 oranges
8–10 oz caster sugar
2 egg whites

2. Slice tops from oranges, scoop out flesh and juice leaving orange shells quite clean.
3. Press orange flesh and juice through sieve and make up to 1 pint with water.
4. Place in pan with sugar. Heat through gently until sugar has dissolved.
5. Simmer for about 5 minutes.
6. Add frozen orange juice, mix well and allow to cool.
7. Place in shallow container and freeze until just set.
8. Whisk egg whites until stiff.
9. Mix egg whites and orange ice together and whisk.
10. Fill orange cups and freeze.
11. Serve straight from freezer as it thaws rapidly.

Note
1. A tangy refreshing sweet.

71

RASPBERRY MERINGUE

Serves 6

Cooking Time: 2–3 minutes
Temperature: Gas No. 7 or 435°F (218°C)

FROM THE FREEZER

1 dairy cream sandwich
8 oz raspberries

1. Use dairy cream sandwich and raspberries from frozen.

FROM THE STORECUPBOARD

2 egg whites
4 oz sugar

2. Remove top round of sponge.
3. Cover cream with raspberries and replace top sponge.
4. Whip egg whites until very stiff. Add 2 oz sugar and beat again.
5. Fold in remaining 2 oz sugar.
6. Spread mixture over top and sides of sponge, so there are no gaps.
7. Place in hot oven for a few minutes to brown meringue.
8. Serve at once.

CRUNCHY RASPBERRY SUNDAE

Serves 4

Cooking Time: None

FROM THE FREEZER

½ pint whipping cream
12 oz raspberries

1. Thaw cream about 2 hours at room temperature.
2. Use raspberries from frozen.

FROM THE STORECUPBOARD

4 oz coconut cookie biscuits
2 tablespoons orange liqueur or brandy

3. Soak biscuits in liqueur for approximately 10 minutes until very mushy.
4. Whip cream and fold into biscuit mixture.
5. Place raspberries in 4 dishes. Add sugar if liked.

6. Pile cream mixture on top and leave in refrigerator for about 2 hours until cream has chilled and raspberries thawed.

Note

1. Freezes well. Fresh cream topping may be prepared and piled on top of any fruit whilst still frozen, and stored in freezer.
2. Storage time in freezer: 2–3 months.

STRAWBERRY CHOUX BUNS

Serves 4

Cooking Time: 35–40 minutes
Temperature: Gas No. 5–6 or 375°–400°F (191°–204°C)

FROM THE FREEZER

¼ pint whipping cream
8 oz strawberries

1. Thaw cream and strawberries about 2 hours at room temperature.

FROM THE STORECUPBOARD

2 oz butter
¼ pint water
2½ oz plain flour
Pinch salt
2 eggs
Icing sugar

2. Melt butter in ¼ pint water and bring to boil.
3. Remove from heat and beat in flour and salt.
4. Return to moderate heat and beat until soft ball forms.
5. Cool slightly and beat in each egg separately until paste is smooth and glossy.
6. Place 4 mounds of paste on greased baking sheet.
7. Bake for 15–20 minutes at Gas No. 6, 400°F (204°C). Reduce temperature to Gas No. 5, 375°F (191°C) for a further 20–25 minutes, until well puffed and golden.
8. Cool on cake rack and make slash in side to release heat.
9. Whip cream until thick.
10. Fill cooled choux buns with cream and fruit.
11. Dust with icing sugar and serve.

Note

1. Choux pastry freezes well.
2. Freeze without filling.
3. Custard may replace cream, and any fruit may replace strawberries.
4. Storage time in freezer: up to 6 months.

MILLE FEUILLES

Serves 4 to 6

Cooking Time: Approximately 10 minutes
Temperature: Gas No. 6 or 400°F (204°C)

FROM THE FREEZER

13½ oz packet puff pastry
½ pint cream
1 lb strawberries or raspberries

1. Thaw pastry and cream about 2 hours at room temperature.
2. Thaw fruit about 1 hour at room temperature.

FROM THE STORECUPBOARD

1 oz caster sugar
Egg glaze
Icing sugar

3. Cut pastry block into 3 even-size pieces.
4. Roll out each piece of pastry very thinly to a roughly circular shape on sugared board.
5. Cut out 1 circle (as large as possible) from each piece of pastry.
6. Place on wetted baking sheet, glaze with beaten egg and bake in fairly hot oven.
7. Carefully remove each circle of pastry and cool.
8. Whip cream until thick.
9. Sandwich together each layer with cream and fruit.
10. Decorate top pastry with piped cream and fruit, and dust with icing sugar.

Note

1. Baked pastry circles may be packed for freezer, but are so fragile that they invariably break.
2. Cream may be prepared as for Pavlova Cake (see page 74).

PAVLOVA CAKE

Serves 4—6

Cooking time: 1 hour
Temperature: Gas No. 3 or 325°F
(163°C)

FROM THE FREEZER

½ pint whipping cream
1 lb strawberries or raspberries

1. Thaw cream about 2 hours at room temperature.
2. Thaw fruit about 1 hour, leaving a few ice crystals to prevent fruit collapsing.

FROM THE STORECUPBOARD

3 egg whites
6 oz caster sugar
½ teaspoon cornflour
½ teaspoon vanilla essence
½ teaspoon lemon juice
2 tablespoons strawberry, raspberry or red currant jam

3. Whisk egg whites until stiff.
4. Gradually add sugar, whisking well between each addition.
5. Fold in cornflour, vanilla essence and lemon juice.
6. Divide pavlova mixture into 3 and spread or pipe each third into similar sized circles on oiled baking sheet.
7. Place in warm oven until firm and pale golden.
8. Whip cream until thick.
9. Carefully coat fruit in jam, reserving a few whole fruit for decoration.
10. Place 1 round of meringue on serving plate.
11. Spread with about one third of cream and top with some of fruit.
12. Repeat with second layer.
13. Top with third meringue. Decorate with piped cream and whole fruit.

Note

1. Tossing fruit in jam helps to keep fruit from collapsing, and thawed fruit from over-moistening meringue.
2. Baked meringue circles may be stored for several weeks in freezer, but will store just as well in air-tight tins.
3. For rapid assembly of this dish, fresh cream may be piped or spread into circles (just like the meringue) and put uncovered into freezer until firm, then wrapped, sealed and stored. Spreading of the cream which may break up very crisp meringue is eliminated.

LEMON HARLEQUINADE

Serves 8 to 10

Cooking Time: None

FROM THE FREEZER

2 lb can or packet melon balls

1. Thaw melon balls overnight in refrigerator or about 2—3 hours at room temperature.

FROM THE STORECUPBOARD

Water
5 lemons
4 oz sugar
2 egg whites, beaten

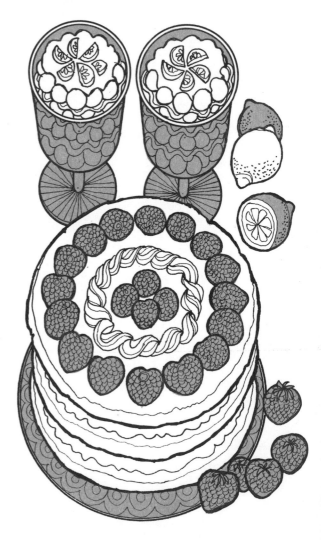

2. Strain syrup from melon balls and make up to 1 pint with water.
3. Add sugar and thinly peeled rind of lemons, and boil for 10 minutes.
4. Allow to cool.
5. Strain to remove lemon rind and add juice of lemons.
6. Put mixture into container suitable for freezing (not too shallow).
7. Place in freezer until almost set.
8. Remove from freezer, fold in stiffly beaten egg whites and return to freezer.
9. After 20 minutes re-stir mixture to keep ice crystals small. Repeat after another 20 minutes.
10. Freeze until firm.
11. Put alternate layers of lemon ice and thawed melon balls in tall wine glasses. Decorate with slices of fresh lemon.
12. Serve immediately, before lemon ice starts to melt.

Note

1. A very refreshing sweet.

FLORIDA COCKTAIL

Serves 8 to 10

Cooking Time: None

FROM THE FREEZER

2 lb melon balls
Segments of 2–3 oranges
Segments of 2–3 grapefruit
2 teaspoons orange juice, undiluted

1. Thaw melon balls overnight in refrigerator or 2–3 hours at room temperature
2. Thaw oranges and grapefruit 1–2 hours at room temperature.
3. Use orange juice from frozen.

FROM THE STORECUPBOARD

3 tablespoons olive oil
3 tablespoons lemon juice
1 tablespoon wine vinegar
Salt and pepper
Chopped mint

4. Drain most of syrup from fruit and combine melon balls with orange and grapefruit segments.

5. Mix together orange juice, oil, lemon juice, vinegar and seasonings, and pour over fruits.
6. Toss fruits gently in dressing.
7. Pile into glasses and sprinkle with chopped mint.
8. Serve chilled.

Note

1. Home frozen melon balls are not very successful. Commercial frozen variety are a very attractive colour.
2. Cocktail may be served either in 2 half melon shells or individual orange or grapefruit shells.
3. Keep melon, orange and grapefruit shells in freezer.

SUMMER PUDDING

Serves 4

Cooking Time: 3–4 minutes

FROM THE FREEZER

4–5 oz cream
Approximately 6 large slices bread
1 lb raspberries
4 oz red currants

1. Thaw cream about 2 hours at room temperature.
2. Thaw bread 5–10 minutes at room temperature.
3. Use raspberries and red currants from frozen.

FROM THE STORECUPBOARD

4 oz sugar

4. Gently heat through fruit with sugar, until sugar has melted and fruits are mixed, about 3–4 minutes.
5. Remove crust from bread and cut to completely line fairly deep dish or 1½ pint basin.
6. Drain fruit and reserve juice.
7. Fill lined dish with fruit and completely cover with lid of bread.
8. Place plate (with 2–3 lb weight on top) which exactly fits top of pudding, over pudding.
9. Chill overnight in refrigerator.
10. Turn out on to shallow serving dish and pour over remaining reserved fruit juice.
11. Serve with thick cream.

STRAWBERRY CHOCOLATE CASES

Serves 4

Cooking Time: None

FROM THE FREEZER

8 oz raspberries or strawberries cream rosettes (see page 29)

1. Use raspberries or strawberries and cream rosettes from frozen.
2. Leave about ½ hour at room temperature before serving.

FROM THE STORECUPBOARD

8 oz plain chocolate
8 paper cake cases

3. Melt chocolate in basin over pan of hot water.
4. Spoon into paper cake cases, making thickish wall around the side. Use 2 paper cases together.
5. Allow to set standing in patty tins.
6. When quite cold and firm, peel away paper.
7. Fill chocolate cases with raspberries or strawberries (or any tinned fruit) and decorate with cream rosettes.

Note

1. Chocolate cases store well in airtight tins.
2. Delicious filled with frozen mousse. Try coffee, topped with cream and a walnut.

RASPBERRY CHEESECAKE

Serves 4 to 6

Cooking Time: None

FROM THE FREEZER

4–5 oz cream
12 oz raspberries

1. Thaw cream about 2 hours at room temperature.
2. Thaw raspberries ½ hour at room temperature.

FROM THE STORECUPBOARD

2 (8 oz) cartons cottage cheese
1 lemon
½ oz powdered gelatine
4 oz caster sugar
2 eggs, separated
6 digestive biscuits, crushed
1 level tablespoon caster sugar
1½ oz butter, melted
Sprigs of mint

3. Well oil 7 inch cake tin with a loose bottom.
4. Retain a few large raspberries in freezer for decoration.
5. Sieve cottage cheese and add to raspberries, with juice and grated rind of lemon.
6. Dissolve gelatine in 2 tablespoons water in small bowl over pan of hot water. Add sugar and blended egg yolks, and stir over hot water until consistency of pouring cream.
7. Allow to cool and when thick but not set, blend into cheese mixture.
8. Whisk cream and fold into cheese mixture.
9. Whisk egg whites until stiff and fold into cheese mixture.
10. Turn into prepared tin and chill until set.
11. Combine biscuits, sugar and melted butter and press down lightly on top of cheesecake. Leave to become firm.
12. Turn out on to 10 inch flat plate. Decorate with whole raspberries and sprigs of mint.

BILBERRY SOUFFLÉ

Serves 6

Cooking Time: 40–45 minutes
Temperature: Gas No. 6 or 400°F (204°C)

FROM THE FREEZER

$\frac{1}{2}$ pint white sauce
8 oz bilberries

1. Thaw sauce by gently heating through.
2. Use bilberries from frozen

FROM THE STORECUPBOARD

Sugar to taste
4 eggs, separated
2 oz caster sugar

3. Well butter 2 pint soufflé dish.
4. Place bilberries and sugar on base.
5. Beat egg yolks and 2 oz sugar into white sauce.
6. Whisk egg whites until just stiff.
7. Fold into sauce.
8. Pour over bilberries.
9. Bake in fairly hot oven.

10. Serve at once when well risen. It will collapse very quickly.

Note

1. Individual soufflés may be made and cooking time reduced to 20–25 minutes.
2. May be frozen uncooked. Spoon bilberries into buttered dish straight from freezer, pour over freshly made soufflé mixture and freeze straight away.
3. Ease out of dish and pack in foil for storage.
4. To bake, unwrap and replace in buttered soufflé dish and bake 50–60 minutes at Gas No. 4 or 350°F (177°C).
5. Storage time in freezer: 4–6 months.

TIPSY PEACHES

Serves 6

Cooking Time: 10–15 minutes
Temperature: Gas No. 4 or 350°F (177°C)

FROM THE FREEZER

6 peach halves
1 arctic roll

1. Thaw peaches 1–2 hours at room temperature.
2. Use arctic roll from frozen.

FROM THE STORECUPBOARD

3 crushed digestive biscuits
3 oz cream cheese
2 tablespoons chopped walnuts
$\frac{1}{2}$ cup white wine

3. Put peaches hollow side up in 2 pint shallow ovenproof dish.
4. Mix together biscuits, cheese and walnuts.
5. Divide evenly to fill peaches and pour wine around.
6. Bake in moderate oven.
7. Place each peach on slice of arctic roll.
8. Pour wine over and serve immediately.

Note

1. If peaches are cooked from frozen, wine will be diluted.

77

PINEAPPLE CREAM

Serves 4

Cooking Time: None

FROM THE FREEZER

5 pineapple rings

1. Use pineapple from frozen.

FROM THE STORECUPBOARD

1 packet pineapple jelly
1 small can evaporated milk
1 tablespoon lemon juice
1 small bar chocolate, grated

2. Break jelly into cubes in 1 pint measure. Pour on boiling water up to $\frac{1}{4}$ pint line. Stir jelly until dissolved.
3. Make up to $\frac{3}{4}$ pint with cold water.
4. Leave until jelly begins to set.
5. Whisk evaporated milk with lemon juice until thick.
6. Place jelly and evaporated milk in large mixing bowl and whisk.
7. Line base of serving dish with 4 pineapple rings and pour on prepared mixture. Leave to set.
8. Cut up remaining pineapple ring and use to decorate dish with grated chocolate.

Note
1. May be frozen.

ROMANOFF STRAWBERRIES

Serves 4

Cooking time: None

FROM THE FREEZER

$\frac{1}{2}$ pint whipping cream
1 lb strawberries
1 tablespoon orange juice, undiluted

1. Thaw cream about 2 hours at room temperature.
2. Thaw strawberries and orange juice $\frac{1}{2}$ hour at room temperature.

FROM THE STORECUPBOARD

1 tablespoon Grand Marnier
Little sugar
1 egg white

3. Leave strawberries for half an hour at room temperature and then cut in half.
4. Place halved strawberries in 4 individual serving glasses with a little sugar, liqueur and orange juice. Leave in refrigerator for about 1 hour.
5. Whip cream with a little sugar until thick.
6. Whisk egg white until just stiff and fold into cream.
7. Pile on to strawberries just before serving.

Dairy Produce & Pastries

DANISH APPLE CAKE

Serves 4

Cooking Time: 5–10 minutes

FROM THE FREEZER

$\frac{1}{2}$ pint whipping cream
4 oz white breadcrumbs

1. Thaw cream about 2 hours at room temperature.
2. Use breadcrumbs from frozen.

FROM THE STORECUPBOARD

1$\frac{1}{2}$ lb cooking apples, peeled, cored and sliced
4 oz caster sugar
2 oz butter
2 tablespoons red currant jelly

3. Cook apples without water until pulped.
4. Add half the sugar and $\frac{1}{2}$ oz butter.
5. Melt remaining butter in frying pan and add breadcrumbs.

6. Cook, stirring, until golden brown colour.
7. Combine breadcrumbs with remaining sugar.
8. Layer apples and crumbs alternately in glass dish, ending with crumbs.
9. Whip cream until thick and pipe or spread on to surface.
10. Decorate with red currant jelly.
11. Chill before serving.

Note

1. This dish can be made with apple purée from freezer.
2. Whole dish may be prepared up to stage 8, cooled and frozen.
3. Storage time in freezer: up to 6 months.

CHOCOLATE REFRIGERATOR CAKE

Serves 6 to 8

Cooking Time: None

FROM THE FREEZER

$\frac{1}{2}$ **pint whipping cream**

1. Thaw cream about 2 hours at room temperature.

FROM THE STORECUPBOARD

Small packet sponge cakes
4 oz plain chocolate
$\frac{1}{4}$ pint milk
1 oz sugar
4 eggs, separated
Flaked almonds, roasted (optional)
2 tablespoons brandy (optional)

2. Slice sponge cakes lengthways and line 2–2$\frac{1}{2}$ pint soufflé dish with half of them.
3. Melt chocolate in pan over hot water, add milk and cook until smooth.
4. Beat sugar with yolks and add to chocolate mixture.
5. Cook until mixture thickens, remove from heat and cool.
6. Whisk egg whites until stiff and fold (with brandy if used) into mixture.
7. Pour half chocolate mixture over sponge cakes, add second layer of sponge cakes and cover in the same

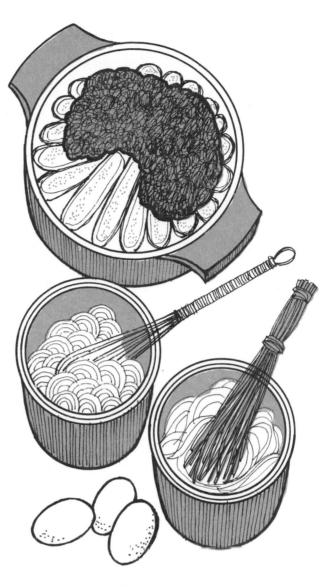

way, pushing cakes down with wooden spoon so that all are covered.
8. Chill in refrigerator for minimum of 12 hours.
9. About 2 hours before serving, turn out of dish.
10. Cover refrigerator cake with whipped cream and sprinkle with flaked roasted almonds (if used).
11. Put into bottom of refrigerator until ready to serve.

Note

1. May be prepared up to and including stage 7, and frozen.
2. Allow to thaw for several hours in refrigerator before serving.
3. Whipped cream may be spread over cake while still frozen.
4. Storage time in freezer: 2–3 months.

ORANGY EGG CUSTARD

Serves 4

Cooking Time: 35–40 minutes
Temperature: Gas No. 3 or 325°F
(163°C)

FROM THE FREEZER

4–5 oz cream
1 orange
2 tablespoons orange juice

1. Thaw cream about 2 hours at room temperature.
2. Thaw orange and juice ½–1 hour at room temperature.

FROM THE STORECUPBOARD

4 eggs
3 oz caster sugar
1 pint milk

3. Whisk eggs and 1 oz sugar together.
4. Warm milk and orange juice, pour on to eggs and whisk again.
5. Pour custard into well buttered 2 pint ovenproof dish and place in baking tin containing warm water.
6. Bake in warm oven until custard has set.
7. Slice orange. Remove rind by cutting around with scissors.
8. Lay orange slices across top of set custard.
9. Sprinkle remaining 2 oz of sugar on top.
10. Place under hot grill until sugar browns.
12. Serve hot or cold, with cream.

GINGER CREAM CUPS

Serves 4

Cooking Time: 2–3 minutes
Temperature: Gas No. 3 or 325°F
(163°C)

FROM THE FREEZER

½ pint whipping cream

1. Thaw cream about 2 hours at room temperature.

FROM THE STORECUPBOARD

8 brandy snaps
2 tablespoons brandy (optional)
4 oz chopped preserved ginger
Grated lemon rind
Flaked almonds

2. Place brandy snaps in warm oven for a few minutes until soft enough to unroll and mould over small upturned teacup.

3. Allow brandy snaps to cool.
4. Carefully ease off teacup.
5. Whip cream until thick and add brandy.
6. Carefully fold in ginger.
7. Pile into brandy snap cases.
8. Decorate with grated lemon rind and almonds.
9. Chill before serving.

Note

1. Brandy snap cases may be home-made and used as above.
2. Cases may be frozen filled or unfilled.
3. Thawing is very quick; best thawed in refrigerator.

CHESTNUT CASTLES

Serves 6

Cooking Time: None

FROM THE FREEZER

1 pint whipping cream

1. Thaw cream about 2 hours at room temperature.

FROM THE STORECUPBOARD

1 egg white
5 oz icing sugar
2 tablespoons rum
¼ teaspoon vanilla essence
8 oz can unsweetened chestnut purée
Slices marron glacé

2. Beat egg white until stiff.
3. Fold in 1 oz icing sugar.
4. Mix half cream with rest of icing sugar.
5. Whisk until floppy consistency.
6. Stir rum and vanilla essence into cream and icing sugar mixture.
7. Fold in chestnut purée and beaten egg white.
8. Divide mixture among 6 quarter-pint cream cartons. Cover with foil and freeze.
9. Remove foil, dip cartons into hot water and invert on serving plate.
10. Decorate while still frozen with rest of cream, whipped to piping consistency, and spread with palette knife, or pipe. Decorate each with slice of marron glacé.

Note

1. Texture will be just right if they are then placed in refrigerator for about 1 hour. If longer than this, put back into freezer and remove to refrigerator 1 hour before serving.

GLACÉ NOËL

Serves 10

Cooking Time: Approximately 10 minutes

FROM THE FREEZER

½ pint whipping cream

1. Thaw cream about 2 hours at room temperature.

FROM THE STORECUPBOARD

1 oz glacé cherries, chopped
1 oz glacé pineapple, chopped
1 oz angelica, chopped
1 oz walnuts, chopped
1 oz flaked almonds
1 oz seeded raisins
1 oz currants
1 oz sultanas
1 oz mixed peel
1 tablespoon brandy
1 tablespoon Madeira
3 egg yolks
1 oz self-raising flour
4 oz caster sugar
½ pint milk

2. Place fruit, nuts, angelica and mixed peel in bowl, and marinate in brandy and Madeira for 1 hour.
3. Beat egg yolks and flour to smooth paste.
4. Dissolve sugar in milk and whisk on to egg yolks.
5. Return to pan to cook flour. Do not allow to boil or egg will curdle.
6. Allow custard to cool.
7. Stiffly whip cream and fold into custard.
8. Add fruit and liquor.
9. Freeze in oiled 2 pint mould.

Note

1. Unmould before start of meal, but keep in freezer until ready to serve.
2. Small portions only will be required as it is very rich.

BANANA SPONGE WITH BUTTERSCOTCH SAUCE

Serves 4 to 6

Cooking Time: None

FROM THE FREEZER

4–5 oz cream
1 dairy cream sandwich

1. Thaw cream about 2 hours at room temperature.
2. Thaw sandwich 1–2 hours in refrigerator.

FROM THE STORECUPBOARD

3 bananas
1 tablespoon lemon juice
3 oz butter
6 oz brown sugar

3. Slice top sponge from cream sandwich as soon as it is taken from freezer.
4. Cut top into 6 portions.
5. Slice bananas and toss in lemon juice to prevent discolouration.
6. Pile bananas on to cream on sandwich base.
7. Arrange 6 sponge portions on bananas in petal fashion.
8. Leave in refrigerator to thaw.
9. Melt butter and sugar slowly in pan.
10. Add cream, bring to boiling point and immediately pour over banana sponge. Serve at once.

ORANGE AND PINEAPPLE BOMBE

Serves 6

Cooking Time: None

FROM THE FREEZER

1 can orange juice
Hawaiian pineapple ice cream
Cream rosettes (see page 29)

FROM THE STORECUPBOARD

4 oz sugar
Grated rind of 1 orange
1 oz blanched almonds, chopped
3 tablespoons Cointreau
Slices of orange and mint leaves

1. Make up orange juice to $\frac{3}{4}$ pint with water.
2. Place in pan with sugar and half the rind. Heat gently until sugar has dissolved.
3. Place in 2 pint basin and freeze for about 1 hour, until thick pulp is formed.
4. Press 1 pint basin into pulp so that mixture is pushed round the sides.
5. Return to freezer for $1\frac{1}{2}$ hours to firm.
6. Remove and ease out inner basin by filling carefully with hot water.
7. Mix almonds and Cointreau into pineapple ice cream and fill centre.
8. Return to freezer for a few minutes to firm up.
9. Put basin upside down on serving dish. Wrap warm wet tea cloth around until released. Decorate with cream rosettes and keep in refrigerator until ready to serve.

Note

1. Careful timing is necessary. It loses its effect if beginning to thaw.

SYLLABUB

Serves 4

Cooking Time: None

FROM THE FREEZER

1 pint whipping cream

1. Thaw cream about 2 hours at room temperature.

FROM THE STORECUPBOARD

2 lemons
$\frac{1}{3}$ pint sherry
Sugar to taste

2. Grate rind from lemons into large bowl.
3. Add lemon juice and sherry, and sugar to taste.
4. Add cream and whisk hard until thick and fluffy.
5. Pile into serving glasses. Chill well before serving.

MACAROON CREAMS

Serves 4–5

Cooking Time: None

FROM THE FREEZER
½ pint whipping cream

1. Thaw cream about 2 hours at room temperature.

FROM THE STORECUPBOARD
2 egg whites
1 oz castor sugar
2 macaroons
1 tablespoon sherry or Madeira
Chopped almonds

2. Whip cream until thick.
3. Whisk egg whites until stiff, add sugar and whisk again.
4. Crush macaroon biscuits in polythene bag with rolling pin.
5. Fold egg whites, macaroons, cream and sherry carefully together.
6. Pile into 4 glasses.
7. Decorate with a few chopped almonds.
8. Chill before serving.

WHISKY CREAMS

Serves 4

Cooking Time: None

FROM THE FREEZER

½ pint whipping cream
Grated lemon rind

1. Thaw cream about 2 hours at room temperature.
2. Use lemon rind from frozen.

FROM THE STORECUPBOARD

½ oz gelatine
¼ pint water
2 tablespoons caster sugar
1 tablespoon whisky
2 egg whites
8 teaspoons fine cut marmalade (whisky-flavoured if possible)
Chopped nuts

3. Dissolve gelatine in water in pan over hot water.
4. Add lemon rind, sugar and whisky, and stir to dissolve sugar.
5. Whip cream stiffly and whisk egg whites until just stiff.
6. Combine cream into gelatine mixture, then fold in egg whites.

7. Place 2 teaspoons marmalade in each of 4 serving glasses.
8. Pour over whisky cream and chill in refrigerator.
9. Serve decorated with chopped nuts.

1. Thaw cream about 2 hours at room temperature.
2. Thaw sauce by gently heating through.
3. Use eclairs from frozen.
4. Cut chocolate eclairs into 3 while still frozen.
5. Pile on to dish or cake stand.
6. Pour over chocolate sauce.
7. Just before serving, trail a little cream over each profiterole for decoration.

Note

1. Chocolate sauce freezes well and is always useful to have in freezer.
2. Real profiteroles are tiny choux pastry buns filled with double cream. See Strawberry Choux Buns for choux pastry recipe (page 72).

NUTTY ICE CREAM FLAN

Serves 4

Cooking Time: 10–15 minutes
Temperature: Gas No. 4 or 350°F (177°C)

FROM THE FREEZER
Vanilla ice cream

1. Use ice cream from frozen.

FROM THE STORECUPBOARD

1 egg
½ teaspoon vanilla essence
4 oz caster sugar
4 oz biscuit crumbs ⎫
4 oz chopped nuts ⎬ **any kind**
Grated chocolate

2. Beat egg until light and fluffy.
3. Fold in all other storecupboard ingredients.
4. Spread into 7 inch flan ring and build up sides.
5. Bake in moderate oven until crisp and dry.
6. Cool, then chill.
7. Pile scoops of ice cream into flan case.
8. Decorate with grated chocolate and serve immediately.

Note

1. Biscuit crust freezes well. Allow to

INSTANT PROFITEROLES

Serves 4

Cooking Time: None

FROM THE FREEZER

4–5 oz cream
½ pint Chocolate Sauce (see page 93)
8 chocolate eclairs

84

cool, then pack carefully in foil. Storage time in freezer: 3–4 months.
2. Thaw about 30 minutes before filling with ice cream.

CHOCOLATE COCONUT CRUNCH

Serves 6

Cooking Time: None

FROM THE FREEZER

Ice cream or mousse

1. Use ice cream or mousse from frozen.

FROM THE STORECUPBOARD

2 oz plain chocolate
1 oz butter
2 tablespoons hot milk
6 oz icing sugar, sieved
12 oz toasted coconut
Grated chocolate or chopped nuts

2. Melt chocolate and butter in basin over pan of hot water.
3. Add hot milk and icing sugar.
4. Blend in coconut.
5. Line base and sides of 8 inch flan ring.
6. Freeze until firm. Remove ring and fill with ice cream or mousse.
7. Decorate with grated chocolate or chopped nuts.
8. Serve immediately.

Note

1. Crust freezes well. Remove flan ring as above and pack carefully. Storage time in freezer: 3–4 months.
2. Thaw about 30 minutes in refrigerator before filling with ice cream or mousse.

IGLOO PUDDING

Serves 4

Cooking Time: 2 minutes
Temperature: Gas No. 8 or 450°F (232°C)

FROM THE FREEZER

1 family block Cornish ice cream

1. Use ice cream from frozen.

FROM THE STORECUPBOARD

6 oz mincemeat
2 egg whites
2 oz caster sugar
Cherries and angelica for decoration

2. Heat mincemeat in small pan to melt suet.
3. Leave until cold.
4. Slice ice cream lengthways into 4, then sandwich together with mincemeat.
5. Place on heatproof plate.
6. Whisk egg whites until stiff and whisk in 1 oz sugar. Fold in remaining sugar.
7. Completely coat ice cream with meringue.
8. Bake in very hot oven.
9. Decorate with cherries and angelica, and serve immediately.

ORANGY-CHOCOLATE MOUSSE

Serves 1

Cooking Time: None

FROM THE FREEZER

1 teaspoon orange juice, undiluted
1 cream rosette (see page 29)

1. Use orange juice and cream rosette from frozen.

FROM THE STORECUPBOARD

1 egg, separated
1 oz chocolate
Chopped nuts

2. Whisk egg white until stiff.
3. Melt chocolate with orange juice in basin over pan of hot water.
4. Beat egg yolk into melted chocolate.
5. Fold in egg white.
6. Allow to set in refrigerator for about 1 hour.
7. Decorate with cream rosette and sprinkle with chopped nuts.

Note

1. Not worth freezing as it takes so little time to make.

ORANGE SOUFFLÉ

Serves 4

Cooking Time: None

FROM THE FREEZER

4 cream rosettes (see page 29)
2 tablespoons cake crumbs
1 tablespoon orange juice,
  undiluted
Grated rind of orange

1. Use cream rosettes, cake crumbs, orange juice and grated orange rind from frozen.

FROM THE STORECUPBOARD

2 tablespoons Grand Marnier or
  Curaçao
2 eggs, separated
2 oz caster sugar

2. Soak cake crumbs in Grand Marnier or Curaçao.
3. Beat egg yolks, orange juice, grated orange rind and sugar until thick.
4. Whisk egg whites until just stiff and fold into yolk mixture.
5. Half fill 4 soufflé dishes with mixture.
6. Place soaked crumbs on top of soufflé mixture.
7. Add remaining soufflé mixture on top.
8. Freeze for 4 hours before serving, topped with cream rosettes.

CARAMEL CRUNCH WITH ICE CREAM

Serves 5 to 6

Cooking Time: None

FROM THE FREEZER

Ice cream (any flavour)

1. Use ice cream from frozen.

FROM THE STORECUPBOARD

4 oz soft brown sugar
½ oz butter
2 oz golden syrup
2 tablespoons water
3 oz cornflakes
Few chopped nuts

2. Gently heat through sugar, butter, syrup and water until sugar has melted. Bring to boil and boil for 3 minutes.
3. Pour mixture over cornflakes mixing quickly to coat flakes.
4. Press lightly into oiled 7 inch ring mould and leave to set.
5. Turn out on serving plate and fill centre with ice cream.
6. Decorate with chopped nuts and serve immediately.

CURRIED APPLE SOUP

Serves 4

Cooking Time: 10–15 minutes

FROM THE FREEZER

4–5 oz cream
¼ pint apple purée
1 pint chicken stock

1. Thaw cream about 2 hours at room temperature.
2. Use apple purée and chicken stock from frozen.

FROM THE STORECUPBOARD

1 oz butter
1 onion, chopped
1 level tablespoon curry powder
1 level tablespoon cornflour
2 egg yolks
1 tablespoon lemon juice
1 eating apple, peeled, cored and diced, tossed in lemon juice
Salt and pepper

3. Fry onion and curry powder in butter.
4. Gently thaw apple purée in chicken stock.
5. Mix cornflour with a little water.
6. Combine onion, apple and cornflour mixture together, and bring to boil.
7. Simmer for 6–7 minutes.
8. Beat egg yolks into cream, stir into apple mixture with seasonings and cook very gently for about 2 minutes.
9. Remove mixture from heat, sieve and chill.
10. Serve pieces of diced apple with each dish of soup.

BAKED EGGS WITH CREAM

Serves 4

Cooking Time: 15 minutes
Temperature: Gas No. 4 or 350°F
(177°C)

FROM THE FREEZER

4–5 oz cream
2 oz grated Cheddar cheese
2 tablespoons buttered crumbs

1. Thaw cream about 2 hours at room temperature.
2. Use cheese and crumbs from frozen.

FROM THE STORECUPBOARD

2 tablespoons lemon juice
2 tablespoons dry white wine
1–2 teaspoons made mustard
Salt and pepper
8 eggs

3. Butter 4 ramekin dishes.
4. Mix together cream, cheese, lemon juice and wine.
5. Add mustard and seasonings.
6. Break 2 eggs into each dish.
7. Cover with cream mixture.
8. Sprinkle with buttered crumbs.
9. Stand dishes in shallow baking tray of water.
10. Bake in moderate oven until eggs are just set. Serve immediately.

POTATO-CREAM BAKE

Serves 4

Cooking Time: 45 minutes
Temperature: Gas No. 4 or 350°F
(177°C)

FROM THE FREEZER

4–5 oz cream

1. Thaw cream about 2 hours at room temperature.

FROM THE STORECUPBOARD

6 medium potatoes
2 oz butter
3 medium onions, finely chopped
Salt
Pepper, freshly ground
¼ pint milk

2. Peel potatoes and cut into very thin slices.
3. Brown onions in 1½ oz butter.
4. Place alternate layers of potatoes and onions in buttered 2 pint oven-proof dish, ending with potato.
5. Sprinkle with salt and pepper and dot with remaining butter.
6. Mix cream with milk and pour half over.

7. Bake in moderate oven until potatoes are cooked.
8. Fifteen minutes before removing from oven pour on remaining cream mixture.

WALNUT SANDWICH WITH COFFEE ICE

Serves 4

Cooking Time: None

FROM THE FREEZER

Coffee ice cream

1. Use ice cream from frozen.

FROM THE STORECUPBOARD

2½ oz butter
2 tablespoons walnuts, finely chopped
4 thin slices of brown bread

2. Cream together chopped nuts and butter.
3. Sandwich between slices of bread.
4. Remove crusts.
5. Chill in refrigerator or freezer until firm.
6. Cut into fingers and serve with ice-cream.

Note

1. May be prepared and frozen. Storage time in freezer: up to 2 months.
2. Thaw for about 10–20 minutes before eating.

MINT FLAVOURED PASTIES

Serves 4

Cooking Time: 20 minutes
Temperature: Gas No. 6 or 400°F (204°C)

FROM THE FREEZER

4–5 oz cream
7½ oz packet shortcrust pastry
2 tablespoons chopped mint
Grated rind of ½ lemon

1. Thaw cream about 2 hours at room temperature.
2. Thaw pastry and mint about 1 hour at room temperature.
3. Use lemon rind from frozen.

FROM THE STORECUPBOARD

4 oz currants
2 oz soft brown sugar
Milk to glaze

4. Roll out pastry thinly.
5. Cut out 6 inch circles.
6. Mix together currants, sugar, mint and lemon rind.
7. Divide mixture between pastry circles.
8. Dampen edges, fold over and seal.
9. Glaze and bake in fairly hot oven.
10. Serve hot or cold, with cream.

BANANA CRISPS

Serves 4

Cooking Time: 12 minutes
Temperature: Gas No. 7 or 425°F (218°C)

FROM THE FREEZER

7½ oz packet puff pastry

1. Thaw pastry 1–2 hours at room temperature.

FROM THE STORECUPBOARD

4 firm bananas, sliced
4 teaspoons lemon juice
2 oz raisins
2 oz demerara sugar
1 oz almonds, blanched and chopped
Milk for glazing

2. Roll pastry to 12 inch square and cut into 4 smaller squares.
3. Mix together bananas, lemon juice, raisins, 1½ oz demerara sugar and almonds.
4. Divide into 4 portions.
5. Spread 1 portion across half one square of pastry from corner to corner.
6. Moisten edges of pastry, fold over to form triangle.
7. Knock-up and flute edges.
8. Repeat with remaining 3 squares of pastry.
9. Brush tops with milk and sprinkle with remaining ½ oz sugar.
10. Bake in hot oven until puffed and golden.

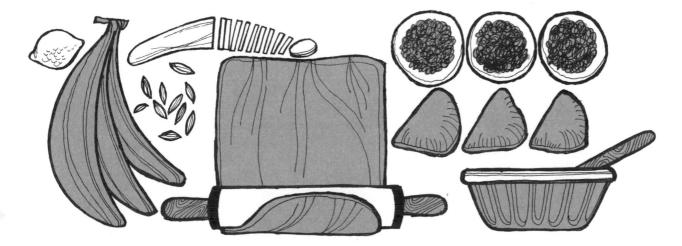

CHOCOLATE TART

Serves 4

Cooking Time: 25–35 minutes
Temperature: Gas No. 6 or 400 °F
(204 °C)

FROM THE FREEZER

7½ oz shortcrust pastry
3 oz breadcrumbs

1. Thaw pastry 1–2 hours at room temperature.
2. Use breadcrumbs from frozen.

FROM THE STORECUPBOARD

4 oz milk
1 oz sugar
2 level teaspoons cocoa
1 egg, beaten
Vanilla essence

3. Line pie plate with pastry, slightly raising edge.
4. Heat milk and dissolve sugar in it.
5. Pour over crumbs and cocoa.
6. Add egg and stir a few minutes.
7. Add vanilla essence and cool slightly.
8. Spread on pastry.
9. Bake in fairly hot oven.

Note

1. May be cooked, cooled and frozen.
2. Storage time in freezer: 3 months.

PINEAPPLE-MINT CREAM

Serves 4

Cooking Time: None

FROM THE FREEZER

½ pint cream

1. Thaw about 2 hours at room temperature.

FROM THE STORECUPBOARD

12 oz tin crushed pineapple
2 tablespoons fresh mint, chopped

2. Whip cream until thick.
3. Drain pineapple.
4. Mix crushed pineapple with chopped mint.
5. Carefully fold into cream.
6. Pile in sundae glasses and chill before serving.

Note

1. This is deliciously refreshing after a rich meal.

Sauces & Savouries

BÉCHAMEL SAUCE

Makes 1 pint

Cooking Time: 5–10 minutes

FROM THE STORECUPBOARD

1 pint milk
½ onion
1 stalk celery
1 sprig thyme
½ bay leaf
6 peppercorns
2 oz butter
2 tablespoons flour
Salt
Grated nutmeg

1. Place onion, celery, herbs and peppercorns in milk, and bring to boil.
2. Set aside for 30 minutes.
3. Melt butter, add flour, and cook for 1 minute.
4. Strain milk and gradually add to roux, stirring all the time.
5. Bring to boil. Add salt and a little grated nutmeg.
6. Simmer 2–3 minutes. Season to taste.
7. Pour into freezer container, leaving 1 inch headspace, and run a little cold milk on top to prevent skin forming. Seal, cool and freeze.

Note

1. This basic white sauce may become cheese, parsley, onion, etc, with appropriate additions.
2. Basic sauce storage time in freezer: 4–6 months.

SWEET AND SOUR SAUCE

Serves 4

Cooking Time: Approximately 10 minutes

FROM THE STORECUPBOARD

8 oz can pineapple
2 small carrots, thinly sliced
1 green pepper, de-seeded and sliced
1 level tablespoon cornflour
1 level tablespoon brown sugar
2–3 teaspoons Soy sauce
2 tablespoons olive oil
2–3 teaspoons vinegar
3–4 pickled onions, gherkins or mixed pickles

1. Drain pineapple into pan. Dice pineapple.
2. Simmer carrot and pepper in pineapple juice for 5 minutes.
3. Mix cornflour, brown sugar, Soy sauce, oil and vinegar together.
4. Blend with pineapple juice in pan.
5. Bring to boil and simmer for 3 minutes.
6. Slice pickles and add with diced pineapple to sauce.
7. Cool and pack in freezer container, leaving 1 inch headspace.

Note

1. To reheat, thaw overnight in refrigerator or heat gently through in saucepan.
2. Storage time in freezer: 2–3 months.

ESPAGNOLE SAUCE

Makes 1 pint

Cooking Time: 1½–2 hours

FROM THE STORECUPBOARD

2 oz green streaky bacon
2 carrots
1 Spanish onion
2 stalks celery

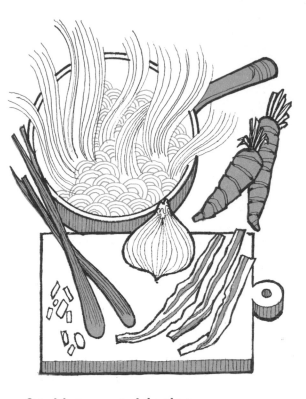

2 tablespoons dripping
1 clove garlic, crushed
2 oz flour
1½ pints beef stock or water
Bouquet garni
3 tablespoons tomato purée

1. Chop bacon, carrots, onion and celery coarsely.
2. Fry in dripping with garlic until golden brown.
3. Add flour and cook slowly until well browned, which may take ½ hour.
4. Add half the stock and stir until sauce thickens.
5. Add remaining stock with bouquet garni and tomato purée, and bring to boil.
6. Simmer very slowly for 1½ hours, stirring frequently.
7. Skim off any fat. Strain through sieve.
8. Pour into freezer container, leaving 1 inch headspace. Seal, cool and freeze.

Note

1. Sauce may be prepared up to and including stage 3 and brown roux frozen. Divide and label roux before packaging.
2. Storage time in freezer: 6 months.

ITALIAN TOMATO SAUCE

Makes 1 pint

Cooking Time: Approximately 35 minutes

FROM THE STORECUPBOARD

2 tablespoons oil
2 onions, chopped
2 sticks celery, chopped
Few bacon rinds
1 clove garlic, crushed
2 lb ripe tomatoes, fresh or canned
2 level tablespoons cornflour
1 pint water or stock
1 level tablespoon brown sugar
$\frac{1}{2}$ level teaspoon basil
Salt and pepper

1. Fry onion, celery, bacon rinds and garlic in oil for 3–4 minutes, without browning.
2. Add roughly chopped tomatoes or canned tomatoes with juice and cook, stirring for 1–2 minutes.
3. Blend cornflour with a little water. Add with remaining water, sugar and basil to pan, and bring to boil.
4. Simmer for about 30 minutes, strain and season to taste.

5. Pour into freezer container. Cool, seal and freeze.

Note

1. *For mixer owners:* Put all ingredients into liquidizer and blend on maximum speed for 30 seconds. Simmer for about 15 minutes.
2. If canned tomatoes are used, it is not necessary to strain sauce to remove skins.
3. Storage time in freezer: 8–10 months.

FRUITY CURRY SAUCE

Makes 1 pint

Cooking Time: Simmer for 25 minutes

FROM THE STORECUPBOARD

1 tablespoon dessicated coconut
2 tablespoons oil
1 large onion, chopped
1 large eating apple, peeled, cored and sliced
1 oz flour
1½ level tablespoons curry powder
1 pint juice from canned pineapples made up with water
2 oz sultanas
2 pineapple rings, chopped
1 tablespoon tomato purée
1 tablespoon marmalade

1. Just cover coconut with boiling water.
2. Leave for 5 minutes, strain and use resulting coconut milk, discarding coconut.
3. Fry onion and apple in oil for 1–2 minutes.
4. Add flour and curry powder, and cook for 5 minutes.
5. This will be a very dry mixture. Keep stirring to prevent burning.
6. Add all other ingredients, including coconut milk, and bring to boil, stirring all the time.
7. Simmer for at least 25 minutes.

Note

1. Cool sauce as quickly as possible (put in sealed polythene container and allow cold water tap to run on it) and freeze. This, like all other curries, is better for reheating.
2. It is more useful to freeze quantities of curry sauce to add to meat, chicken, shell fish, etc., rather than having quantities of curried beef, lamb, etc.
3. This is not a very hot curry sauce, and is particularly good with fish or with hard-boiled eggs. Hard-boil fresh eggs, shell and heat through in sauce.
4. Storage time in freezer: 3–4 months.

CHOCOLATE SAUCE

Serves 4

Cooking Time: 20 minutes

FROM THE STORECUPBOARD

4 oz plain chocolate
4 oz butter
1 oz granulated sugar
¼ pint water

1. Place all ingredients in pan and heat gently until sugar has dissolved.
2. Simmer until slightly thickened. Do **not** boil.
3. Pour into freezer container and freeze.

Note

1. Thaw slowly, reheat and serve.
2. Storage time in freezer: 2–3 months.

QUICK CHOCOLATE SAUCE

Serves 4

Cooking Time: 5 minutes

FROM THE STORECUPBOARD

6 oz soft brown sugar
2–3 oz cocoa
1 oz dried milk
½ pint water
Few drops vanilla essence

1. Place all ingredients in pan and stir until sugar has dissolved.
2. Boil gently for about 5 minutes to thicken.
3. Remove from heat and allow to cool.
4. Pour into freezer container, leaving 1 inch headspace. Seal and freeze.

Note

1. Storage time in freezer: 2–3 months.

BARBEQUE SAUCE

Serves 4

Cooking Time: 30 minutes

FROM THE STORECUPBOARD

1 oz butter
2 oz onion, chopped
2 oz celery, chopped
½ level tablespoon plain flour
½ level teaspoon paprika
1 level teaspoon salt
1 tablespoon lemon juice
¼ pint water
2 oz soft brown sugar
⅛ pint vinegar
1 green pepper, chopped (optional)
1 tablespoon chilli sauce
1 tablespoon Worcestershire sauce
1 tablespoon tomato ketchup
1 tablespoon made mustard

1. Lightly fry onion and celery in butter.
2. Add all other ingredients in above order.
3. Simmer for 30 minutes. Stir occasionally.

Note

1. A handful of chopped peppers from freezer may be used instead of fresh. Add to made sauce when reheating sauce before serving.
2. Serve with pork chops, pork spare ribs, chicken, etc.
3. Storage time in freezer: 2–3 months.

FRENCH ONION BREAD

Serves 4 to 6

Cooking Time: 40 minutes
Temperature: Gas No. 4 or 350°F (177°C)

FROM THE STORECUPBOARD

4 oz butter
1 pint packet onion soup mix
1 long French loaf

1. Soften butter and add onion soup mix.
2. Cut loaf in half lengthways and spread with butter mixture.
3. Wrap in foil and freeze.

4. Bake straight from freezer in moderate oven.
5. Open up foil for further 10 minutes to crisp.

Note

1. Storage time in freezer: 1 week. Crusts begin to shell off if stored for longer.

OLIVE CHEESE CANAPÉS

Makes 24

Cooking Time: 10 minutes
Temperature: Gas No. 6 or 400°F (204°C)

FROM THE FREEZER

½ lb grated Cheddar cheese

1. Use cheese from frozen.

FROM THE STORECUPBOARD

2 oz softened butter
4 oz flour
½ level teaspoon paprika
1 jar pimento stuffed olives (24)

2. Mix grated cheese and butter together.
3. Blend in flour and paprika.
4. Shape about 1 tablespoon round each olive. Keep dipping hands in flour to stop sticking.
5. Place on greased baking sheet and bake in fairly hot oven.
6. Serve hot or cold.

Note

1. May be prepared up to baking stage, cooled and frozen.
2. Bake from frozen for 20 minutes.
3. Storage time in freezer: 2–3 months.

CHEESE BREAD

Serves 6

Cooking Time: 5–10 minutes
Temperature: Gas No. 7 or 425°F (218°C)

FROM THE FREEZER

6 thin slices of white bread
3 oz grated Cheddar cheese

1. Use bread and cheese from frozen.

FROM THE STORECUPBOARD

2 oz butter, softened
1 egg white

2. Remove crusts from bread and lightly spread with butter.
3. Whisk egg white until stiff and fold in grated cheese.
4. Spread mixture evenly over 6 slices of bread.
5. Bake in hot oven until golden brown crust has formed.
6. Serve with Spinach Soup (see page 68).

SAVOURY TWIRLS

Makes about 24

Cooking Time: 15 minutes
Temperature: Gas No. 6 or 400 °F (204 °C)

FROM THE FREEZER

7$\frac{1}{2}$ oz packet shortcrust pastry

1. Thaw pastry about 1 hour at room temperature.

FROM THE STORECUPBOARD

3 oz ham, chopped
2 level teaspoons made mustard
2 teaspoons chopped pickle

2. Roll out pastry very thinly.
3. Mix together ham, mustard, and pickle, and spread over pastry.
4. Roll up as for Swiss roll. Chill in freezer for 10 minutes.
5. Slice very thinly and bake in fairly hot oven.

CHEESE SOUFFLÉ WITH GARLIC CROÛTONS

Serves 4

Cooking Time: 40–45 minutes
Temperature: Gas No. 6 or 400 °F (204 °C)

FROM THE FREEZER

$\frac{1}{2}$ pint Béchamel Sauce (see page 90)
5 oz grated Cheddar cheese
4 tablespoons garlic croûtons

1. Thaw sauce by standing container in hot water, then reheat gently in saucepan.
2. Use cheese and croûtons from frozen.

FROM THE STORECUPBOARD

6 eggs, separated
Salt and pepper
$\frac{1}{2}$ level teaspoon made mustard

3. Thaw Béchamel sauce over low heat, stirring all the time.
4. Bring to boil and add grated cheese, seasonings and mustard.
5. Cook gently until cheese has completely melted.
6. Remove from heat and add egg yolks one at a time.
7. Whisk egg whites until just stiff.
8. Fold egg whites and croûtons carefully into cheese sauce.
9. Pile into buttered 2 pint soufflé dish, and bake in fairly hot oven until golden and well risen.
10. Eat immediately.

INDEX OF RECIPES